Telling the Untold
STORIES

Telling the Untold STORIES

Encounters with the Resurrected Jesus

John Beverley Butcher

TRINITY PRESS INTERNATIONAL
Harrisburg, Pennsylvania

Trinity Press International, P.O. Box 1321, Harrisburg, PA 17105
Trinity Press International is a division of the Morehouse Group.

Cover art: *Let There Be Light* © 1997 James Disney. Reproduced courtesy of James Disney. Reproductions are available from Bridge Building Images, Inc., www.BridgeBuilding.com, 1-800-325-6263, or PO Box 1048, Burlington, VT 05402-1048.

Cover design: Wesley Hoke

Library of Congress Cataloging-in-Publication Data
Butcher, John Beverley.
    Telling the untold stories : encounters with the resurrected Jesus / John Beverley Butcher.
        p. cm.
    Includes bibliographical references (p.) and index.
    ISBN 1-56338-348-9
        1. Jesus Christ—Appearances. I. Title.

BT490.B88 2001
232.9'7–dc21   00-046689

Printed in the United States of America
00 01 02 03 04 05   10 9 8 7 6 5 4 3 2 1

I dedicate this book to my granddaughter, Suraya Noor Elizabeth Essi, born to my daughter, Marie Butcher, and Maher Essi on April Fool's Day 1997. May the foolishness of these outrageous stories bring her wisdom. May she come to know the Resurrected Jesus and experience her own resurrection in heart, mind, body, and soul. These are my dearest hopes for Suraya and for you, the reader.

"The Seed of True Humanity is within you."
The Gospel of Mary (Magdalene)

Contents

Abbreviations

JB	Jerusalem Bible
KJV	King James Version
NHL	Nag Hammadi Library
NJB	New Jerusalem Bible
NRSV	New Revised Standard Version
RSV	Revised Standard Version
SV	Scholars Version

Introduction

For two thousand years there has been a wide variety of thought, opinion, and experience regarding the meaning of the resurrection of Jesus. Many have called the event a pious hoax. For others, the resurrection is a living reality. Although countless books have been written on the subject, we are no closer now to a definitive view of the topic than we have ever been.

In the middle of the twentieth century, several discoveries provided new materials that offer accounts of the resurrection beyond those in the New Testament.

Although many people have heard about the Dead Sea Scrolls, they may not be familiar with the Nag Hammadi Library, which was discovered in 1945. Muhammad Ali, not the fighter but a farmer, and his brother Khalifah, digging near their hometown of Nag Hammadi for fertilizer, unearthed a large earthenware jar containing thirteen leather-bound books.

The books in the Nag Hammadi Library were probably buried about the beginning of the fourth century C.E. in order to protect and preserve them. The forty-five documents in this collection were written in Coptic and are copies of originals that come from the first through the third century C.E. Included in this library are books with sayings attributed to Jesus (*The Gospel of Thomas* and *The Dialogue of the Savior*), and a first-century Gospel named for a woman (*The Gospel of Mary*).

What is most exciting is that the collection contains twelve books that provide written documentation for encounters of people with the Resurrected Jesus. These stories offer new information about ways that the family, friends, and followers of Jesus reacted to his death, experienced his resurrection, and formed communities after his death.

The major resurrection stories have never been collected and placed in one volume. In this book, the recently discovered stories of the Resurrected Jesus are added to those from the New Testament to reveal more of the varieties of resurrection experience.

In my writing, I use the name *Jesus* to refer to the historic person who was born of Mary, grew up in Nazareth, was baptized by John, and began his ministry of teaching and healing until he was publicly executed. The life story of Jesus is clothed in rich symbolism. Historic and symbolic material are also interwoven in telling the stories of encounters with the Resurrected Jesus.

The Mystery of the resurrection raises many questions: Where do we see continuities between the historic Jesus and the Resurrected Jesus? Where might the stories reveal discontinuities? What might be the relationship between the historic Jesus and the Risen Christ? How might the evidence contained in these first-century stories help us experience resurrection in the twenty-first?

1

Mary Magdalene,
Traveling Companion of Jesus

In the Synoptic Gospels, Mary Magdalene, along with Mary, the mother of James, makes a visit to Jesus' tomb to complete his burial rites. Before they get to the burial place, they wonder who will help them roll away the stone that blocks the entrance to the tomb. When they arrive, they find a heavenly messenger (Matthew's gospel account) or a young man clothed in white (Mark's gospel account) telling them that Jesus has been raised. In Matthew's Gospel, they flee and tell the other disciples, who do not listen. In Mark's Gospel, the women flee and do not tell anyone what they have seen.

Who is Mary Magdalene and what do we know about her? A very common impression is that she is a prostitute. Films like *The Last Temptation of Christ*, *Jesus Christ Superstar*, and numerous others reinforce this mistaken identity. Nowhere in the early records is there any evidence that she was a prostitute.

The assailing of her character comes in the sermons of Gregory the Great, who became pope in 590 C.E. He mistakenly identified Mary of Magdala, Mary of Bethany, and the unnamed "sinful woman" in the Gospel of Luke as being one and the same person. Thereafter, Mary Magdalene was seen as a prostitute. When someone's reputation has been smeared for many hundreds of years, it can be difficult to clear her name. A careful study of all the evidence will allow a fresh understanding of her character to emerge.

In the New Testament Gospels, we learn that Mary is from Magdala, a small fishing village on the western shore of the sea of Galilee. Her name is first mentioned in the Gospel of Luke: Jesus "went on through cities and villages, proclaiming and bringing the good news of the kingdom of God. The twelve were with him, as well as some women who had been cured of evil spirits and infirmities: Mary, called Magdalene, from whom seven demons had gone out, and Joanna, the wife of Herod's steward Chuza, and Susanna, and many others, who provided for them out of their resources" (Luke 8:1–3, NRSV).

When and where did Mary and Jesus first meet? Had they known each other prior to her experience of healing? Had she heard about him from others and decided to see for herself? What might have drawn her to him originally? What might she have hoped to receive from him? How might Jesus have felt about her at first?

Who or what might have been the "seven demons" that took their leave from Mary? Our vocabulary today is quite different from that of people in the first century. We are not likely to complain of problems with "demons." Even if someone feels gripped by some sort of "evil spirit," one would rarely express it that way for fear of being considered really crazy.

Today, when people go to therapists, analysts, counselors, and priests, they are more likely to state their symptoms in terms of anxiety attacks, depression, or stress. Whatever the disturbing feelings might be, our main concern is to have them go away. Sometimes we resist facing the issues behind the symptoms, but sooner or later we begin to realize that our symptoms will not disappear until we are willing to struggle with our relationships and the dynamics of our inner world. Sometimes a therapeutic relationship enables us to work through the underlying dis-ease that is producing the symptoms.

So how might Mary have become free of her seven symptoms? Does Jesus "heal" her? Or does he enable her to be in touch with her own inner strengths that bring about her healing? Whatever occurs for Mary, we know that afterwards she starts traveling with Jesus. Is it out of gratitude that she wants to be with him? Does she ask if she might come along? Does Jesus invite her to travel with him? Or might they together sense that this is the right thing to do?

Mary and the other women provide for Jesus and the Twelve "from their resources." Clearly, the women are supporting the men, not the other way around. We know very little about Mary's background and her resources. The Gospels can be quite tantalizing and frustrating because of the information that is not included, particularly regarding the lives of the women.

According to the *The Gospel of Philip*, "There were three who always walked with the Lord: Mary his mother and her sister and Magdalene, the one who was called his companion" (Gospel of Philip 59:8–9, NHL).

A little later in the same Gospel we find: "The companion of the Savior is Mary Magdalene. But Christ loved her more than all the disciples and used to kiss her often on her mouth. The rest of the disciples were offended by it and expressed disapproval. They said to him, 'Why do you love her more than all of us?' The Savior answered and said to them, 'Why do I not love you like her?'" (Gospel of Philip 63:33—64:5, NHL). As often occurs in the Gospels, Jesus answers a question by asking another!

In the *The Gospel of Mary*, "Peter said to Mary, 'Sister, we know that the Savior loved you more than any other woman'" (Gospel of Mary 6:1, SV).

Mary Magdalene at the Cross

During the crucifixion of Jesus: "Now some women were observing this from a distance, among whom were Mary of Magdala, and Mary the Mother of James the younger and Joses, and Salome. These women had regularly followed him and assisted him when he was in Galilee, along with many other women who had come to Jerusalem in his company" (Mark 15:40–41, SV). All four New Testament Gospels indicate that Mary Magdalene is at the cross; she stays with Jesus to the very end.

The scene of Jesus' crucifixion is desolate. In the last moments of his life, Jesus is powerless and abandoned by God. *The Gospel of Peter* tells the story this way: "It was midday and darkness covered the whole of Judea. They were confused and anxious for fear the sun had set since he was still alive. For it is written that, 'The sun must not set upon one who has been executed.' And one of them said, 'Give him vinegar with something bitter to drink.' And they mixed it and gave it to him to drink. And they fulfilled all things and brought to completion the sins on their head. Now many went about with lamps, and, thinking it was night, they laid down. And the Lord cried out, saying, 'My power, my power, you have abandoned me!' When he said this, he was taken up. And at that moment, the veil of the Jerusalem temple was torn in two" (Gospel of Peter 5:1–6, SV).

Mark tells us that Jesus cries, "My God, my God, why have you forsaken me?" (Mark 15:34, NRSV). Job, in his deepest agonies, is able to say, "Though he slay me, yet will I trust in him" (Job 13:15, KJV). In Job-like fashion, Jesus in his darkest hour cries out, "Father, into your hands I commend my spirit" (Luke 23:46, NRSV).

We can only begin to imagine how Mary Magdalene feels as she sees Jesus suffering and hears him crying out that God has abandoned him. Yet she remains with him even to his final breath, his letting go of life, and his excruciatingly painful death.

The symbolic details in the story of the crucifixion provide rich meaning and point us to deeper understanding. For example, at the moment when Jesus dies, the veil of the Temple is torn in two. The veil that hid the Mystery of God is ripped apart and the heart of God is exposed for those who have eyes to see.

The scene in which Jesus' body is taken from the cross has inspired many painters and sculptors who bring out even more of the symbolic meaning. For example, a careful look at Michelangelo's *Pietà* and the woman holding his body raises questions: Does she appear to be a generation older than Jesus, or is she of similar age? Who is this woman, really? Is she Mary his mother, or might this be Mary Magdalene? Or might the sculpture embody both possibilities?

Artistic representations such as the *Pietà* express visually the feelings and care given to the beloved dead by those who remain.

Mary Magdalene's Experience with the Resurrected Jesus

Just as all the Gospel writers agree that Mary Magdalene is present at the death of Jesus, so they all name her in their resurrection stories. The names of the other women vary.

Mark 16:1 names Mary Magdalene, Mary the mother of James, and Salome. Luke 24:10 has Mary Magdalene, Joanna, Mary the mother of James, and the other women. Matthew 28:1 names Mary Magdalene and the other Mary. *The Gospel of Peter* 9:12 (SV) has "Mary Magdalene and her women friends."

Probably the most fascinating story is in the Gospel of John where Mary Magdalene has a conversation with the Risen Christ. In all of the stories, the tomb itself is empty. In John, Mary turns away from the tomb and walks into a garden, where she meets someone whom she imagines to be the gardener. He asks her, "Woman, why are you crying? Who is it you're looking for?" and Mary replies, "Please, mister, if you moved him, tell me where you have put him so I can take him away" (John 20:15, SV).

Then Jesus calls her by name, "Mary." She turns and says to him in Hebrew, "Rabboni," which means "Teacher." Jesus tells her, "Don't touch me because I have not yet gone to the Father. But go to my brothers and tell them this: 'I'm going back to my Father and your Father—to my God and your God.'"

Mary of Magdala goes and reports to the disciples, "I have seen the Master," and relates everything he had told her (John 20:16–18, SV).

How might Mary's initial nonrecognition shift to become her first encounter with the Resurrected Jesus? Does her awareness come by hearing her name called by a familiar voice? Is this an intense outer vision or a deep inner realization of the continuing presence of Jesus within her?

This garden encounter is but the first of many more to come.

2

Searching for the Parents
of the Historic Jesus

Two kinds of truth, historic and symbolic, are woven into the stories of Jesus' life. The stories of his birth have tremendous meaning in what they say about Jesus and also about our own inner life.[1]

Historically, who are the parents of Jesus? There seems little or no reason to doubt that Mary was, in fact, the mother of the historic Jesus. However, when we begin looking for his father, our search takes us in a very different direction.

One interpretation says that the birth stories are historic fact. Jesus had no earthly father. God was his Father and Joseph his foster father. Another interpretation says that Jesus was conceived and born in the usual way as a result of his parents' having made love nine months previously.

In Luke 4:22, Jesus is referred to as "Joseph's son." Aside from the birth stories and this one phrase, Joseph is never mentioned again in the Gospels, the Book of Acts, or anywhere else in the entire New Testament.

So who is this Joseph, then? Where does he come from? What happens to him? Why does he disappear from the scene?

In the Hebrew Scriptures, Joseph is a very significant character. The lives of the people of Israel are in danger because of severe famine. They make the long trek into Egypt, where the Pharaoh has placed Joseph in authority with responsibilities for the storehouses and food distribution. Joseph is in position to provide food for the rest of the Israelites.

Similarly, in the Gospel stories, the Child's life is in danger because of Herod the King's order to kill all male infants. Another Joseph saves the Child and his mother by taking them safely to Egypt. Later, he brings them back home when the danger is past, just as the Israelites eventually made their exodus from Egypt and entered the promised land.

At the symbolic level, the history of the Israelite people is retold in the life of Jesus, who embodies the new Israel. As part of the story, the name of Joseph carries much symbolic meaning. Is there any evidence of his being a historic person as well?

Perhaps we can discover more about the historic Joseph by searching for Jesus' brothers and sisters. Mark provides a scene where Jesus comes into his hometown with his disciples. On the Sabbath, Jesus begins teaching in the synagogue, and many who hear him are astounded. They say, "Where's he getting this?" and "What's the source of all this wisdom?" and "Who gave him the right to perform such miracles? This is the carpenter, isn't it? Isn't he Mary's son? And who are his brothers, if not James and Judas and Simon? And who are his sisters, if not our neighbors?" (Mark 6:2–3, SV). Mark tells us that Jesus has siblings and provides the names of his brothers, but not his sisters.

Matthew's version reads, "This is the carpenter's son, isn't it?" (Matt. 13:55, SV). So who is the carpenter: Jesus or his father? One way around the question is to say that they both were carpenters and that the son learned the trade from his father.

At the scene of the crucifixion, Jesus' mother; his mother's sister Mary, the wife of Clopas; and Mary Magdala stood by the cross (John 19:25). Would Mary have a sister also named Mary? Would parents give the same name to two daughters? What is going on here?

John tells us that Mary's sister is the wife of Clopas (John 19:25, NRSV).

Mark says that Mary Magdalene is at the cross with Mary, "the mother of James the younger and of Joses, and Salome" (Mark 15:40). So where is Mary, the mother of Jesus? She is right there in front of us. She is mentioned as the mother of Jesus' brothers and sisters, but not as his mother.

At this point Mark does not identify this Mary as the mother of Jesus: but as we have already seen, Mark does say that Jesus is son of Mary and brother of James and Joses and Judas and Simon. So, is not this Mary Jesus' mother? And have we not just now learned the name of one of his sisters, Salome?

By the end of the first century, the virgin birth stories were circulating, and the virginity of Mary was being emphasized more and more, finally climaxing in the teachings of Jerome, who in 383 C.E. writes a lengthy and carefully argued treatise entitled "The Perpetual Virginity of Mary."

There may be a simple explanation for the story's having two sisters, both named Mary. Mythic truth may be overwhelming and hiding some of the historic truth. In other words, in an effort to assert the meaning of the virgin birth stories, the historic details of Jesus' family, his parents and siblings, are becoming obscured.

Let's try to put some puzzle pieces together and see if they fit. Suppose Mary's sister, Mary, is an invention of the Gospel writer. Instead of two Marys, what we really have is one Mary who is the mother of Jesus and the wife of Clopas. If this is the case, then Mary and Clopas are the parents of James and Joses, and Judas and Simon and Salome and the other sisters of Jesus.[2]

A Father's Experience of His Risen Son?

In Luke 24:13–35, the Resurrected Jesus appears to someone named "Cleopas" and one other person. The two are walking from Jerusalem to Emmaus. Who is this Cleopas? Nowhere else in the Scriptures is this name with this spelling mentioned. Is it possible that Clopas, the husband of Mary's "sister," is one and the same as Cleopas?

Robert Eisenman points out that "'Clopas,' 'Cleopas,' 'Cleophas,' and 'Alphaeus' are simply Jesus' father Joseph."[3]

If Clopas and Cleopas are the same person, then the Gospel of Luke provides us with a resurrection story featuring Jesus' father and someone else. Might the other person be his wife, Mary? If this is the case, then this resurrection story is about the parents of Jesus experiencing their risen son.

On the other hand, maybe this is not Mary with Cleopas but possibly one of his other sons—James, for example. According to Origen (ca. 185–254 C.E.), the other person with Cleopas is Simon.[4] If this is the case, then we have an interesting discovery: on the first Easter afternoon, the characters walking along together are Jesus' brother Simon and their father, Cleopas: "Now on the same day two of them were going to a village called Emmaus, about seven miles from Jerusalem" (Luke 24:13, NRSV).

Interestingly, the name *Emmaus* in Greek means "hot spring" or "hot well." I can certainly understand why anyone who had been through the grueling events of the trials, torture, and crucifixion of Jesus might have wanted to get away from it all and head for the healing waters of natural hot springs.

On their way to this place of healing, these two are talking with each other about all the things that have happened. Jesus himself comes near and walks with them, but their eyes are kept from recognizing him.

> And he said to them, "What are you discussing with each other while you walk along?" They stood still, looking sad. Then one of them, whose name was Cleopas, answered him, "Are you the only stranger in Jerusalem who does not know the things that have taken place there in these days?" He asked them, "What things?" They replied "The things about Jesus of Nazareth, who was a prophet mighty in deed and word before God and all the people, and how our chief priests and leaders handed him over to be condemned to death and crucified him. But we had hoped that he was the one to redeem Israel. Yes, and besides all this, it is now the third day since these things took place. Moreover, some women of our group astounded us. They were at the tomb early this morning, and when they did not find his body

there, they came back and told us that they had indeed seen a vision
of angels who said that he was alive. Some of those who were with us
went to the tomb and found it just as the women had said; but they
did not see him." Then he said to them, "Oh, how foolish you are, and
how slow of heart to believe all that the prophets have declared! Was it
not necessary that the Messiah should suffer these things and then
enter into his glory?" Then beginning with Moses and all the prophets,
he interpreted to them the things about himself in all the scriptures.

As they came near the village to which they were going, he walked
ahead as if he were going on. But they urged him strongly, saying, "Stay
with us, because it is almost evening and the day is now nearly over." So
he went in to stay with them. When he was at the table with them, he
took bread, blessed and broke it, and gave it to them. Then their eyes
were opened, and they recognized him; and he vanished from their
sight. They said to each other, "Were not our hearts burning within us
while he was talking to us on the road, while he was opening the scriptures to us?" That same hour they got up and returned to Jerusalem;
and they found the eleven and their companions gathered together.
They were saying, "The Lord has risen indeed, and he has appeared to
Simon!" Then they told what had happened on the road, and how he
had been made known to them in the breaking of the bread.

(Luke 24:13–35, NRSV).

In the stranger, Cleopas and his companion discover the Resurrected Jesus
in three ways: through conversation as they walked along, through having the
Scriptures carefully explained to them, and through sharing bread.

Jesus' father, whether he is named Joseph or Cleopas or both, and his
mother, Mary, would have seen their son grow up, become an adult, and take
on the carpenter's trade. Around the age of thirty, their son Jesus is baptized and
has a profound experience that redirects him into a new way of life. His ministry
begins, and he soon becomes known as a teacher and healer. What might it
have been like for this father and mother to see large numbers of people
drawn to their son, only to see him the object of growing resistance and opposition? And how might they have felt as their son is identified by the authorities as a dangerous person? And then what agony must they have felt as their
son is arrested, tried, and sentenced to death?

Most parents want to see their children grow up healthy, happy, and fulfilled. Most parents expect to die before their children do. It is a shock when a
child dies first. It is even more of a shock when a son runs afoul of the law—
still worse to see a son publicly executed. Can you imagine what it would be
like to be the parents of someone killed by the state through capital punishment?

Before, during, and after the execution, parents might be crying: "My son, my son! What are they doing to my son? What has he done? What have I done that he ends up this way? Why is this happening?"

Likewise, can we imagine what it would be like to try to return to some ordinary activities: going for a walk, sitting down for a simple meal, or trying to get some comfort out of holy writings? Often it is in the ordinary everyday things in familiar places that we begin to experience the presence of a loved one.

You will notice here in this story some very clear eucharistic elements. Whenever people gather, share Scriptures, talk about their lives, and break bread, there is the very real possibility that they will experience something of the Risen Christ with them and in one another.

Ever since Emmaus, countless numbers of people have come to experience that the eucharistic meal is a sharing with the Resurrected Jesus who continues to feed us and strengthen us for daily living.

A Mother's Experience of Her Risen Son?

Because Mary, the mother of Jesus, is such a key figure, we might expect to find some record, either historic or mythic, of her experiences of her risen son. However, as I search through all the resurrection stories available, I have been unsuccessful in finding one attributed specifically to Mary, mother of Jesus. We are left looking for her in the company of others.

For example, Mary may have been present with Jesus and his friends during his last meal. The next day, the Gospels tell us, she is standing at the foot of the cross during his agonizing death. John adds this conversation: "When Jesus saw his mother and the disciple whom he loved standing beside her, he said to his mother, "Woman, here is your son." Then he said to the disciple, "Here is your mother" (John 19:26–27a, NRSV).

Luke tells us that right after the experience of the ascension, the disciples return to Jerusalem, and when they reach the city they go to the upper room where the Eleven join in continuous prayer with several women, including Mary, the mother of Jesus.

Next follows Luke's story of Pentecost, and all are together in one room, possibly the same upper room. There is no specific reference to Mary, the mother of Jesus, being present. However, we might very well assume that she is still meeting with the closest friends of Jesus and is there along with other women and men on the day of Pentecost.

3

James,
Oldest Brother of Jesus

Of all Jesus' siblings, his brother James is the most prominent. Both Mark and Paul refer to James as the brother of Jesus (Mark 6:3, Gal 1:19). Early historians write of James as the brother of Jesus. Josephus, the Jewish historian (37–96 C.E.), describes James as "the brother of Jesus who was called the Christ."[1] Eusebius (260–340 C.E.) writes: "Now the throne of James, who was the first to receive from the Saviour and the apostles the episcopate of the church at Jerusalem, who also as the divine books show, was called a brother of Christ."[2]

At birth, both sons were dedicated to God by their mother and father. James becomes a high priest in Jerusalem, whereas Jesus is an itinerant teacher based in Capernaum and working primarily in Galilee.

James is a leader among the "Ebionim," the poor of the city, whereas Jesus is living and teaching among the poor out in the country. So in one sense both brothers have a similar ministry among poor people, but how are their teachings similar and how are they different?

Both brothers have a perspective and teaching that clashes with the power structure of the time. James is in the thick of things in Jerusalem, and we might expect to see pressure against him building more rapidly than the pressures against Jesus out in the country.

James is proclaiming that the rule of God will come when the people are freed from foreign occupation. Jesus announces that the kingdom has already come and may be discovered within you. "The Father's imperial rule is inside you and outside you" (Gospel of Thomas 3, SV). The two teachings could be seen as complementary: one giving attention to the outer world, the other to the inner. However, Jesus and James seem to have difficulty understanding each other, and friction develops between them.

Most of us have probably grown up with the impression that Jesus was Mary's firstborn and that any brothers and sisters would have been born after him. However, the lists of brothers often begin with James, then Simon, then Judas, then Joses—who may very well have been Jesus. In other words, James may have been the oldest and Jesus the youngest of the brothers.

If that is the case, then the stories that Jesus tells about brothers take on new meaning. Jesus tells the story of two sons in which the younger brother asks for his share of the inheritance and goes off to explore on his own while the older brother remains home to do the work (Luke 15:11–32). Commonly, this is known as the Parable of the Prodigal Son, but if you look closely you will find the word *prodigal* does not appear in the story; it is only a title put on the story by translators of the King James version. Might this story have originated from Jesus' experience in his own family, where James, the older brother, remains in Jerusalem doing what is expected while Jesus leaves for his wandering journey in the country?

In the time of Jesus, Jerusalem is controlled by the Romans. Some of the Jewish priests work in cooperation with the Roman authorities. Others, like James, are secretly working with the Zealots, who plan and stage revolts with the clear purpose of driving the Romans out of town. Because of James' intense dedication, he is called "James the Just." As an opposition leader, he sides, not with the rich who are in collaboration with the Romans, but with the poor.

James remains primarily in one place—Jerusalem. Apparently, Jesus rarely goes to Jerusalem except several times a year for the festivals of Passover, Pentecost, and Tabernacles. The rest of the time we see Jesus in the region of Galilee as an itinerant teacher moving about from town to town with his closest disciples, both women and men.

The teaching of Jesus centers in proclaiming what has been translated into English as "The Kingdom of the Father," "The Kingdom of God," "The Kingdom of Heaven." In no instance does he define what he means, but he insists that it is here, now, and it is time to become aware of it, to see it, and to cooperate with it. "I shall give you what no eye has seen and what no ear has heard and what no hand has touched and what has never occurred to the human mind" (Gospel of Thomas 17, NHL).

Jesus teaches by illustrating from experiences of people in ordinary life: fishing, farming, baking, and cleaning. He illustrates with relationships between children and parents, adults and children, landowners and peasants. And he continually points to nature: birds of the air, fish of the sea, flowers of the field—common experiences that have meaning hidden within them that all can see, provided they have eyes to see and ears to hear.

Jesus deals directly with birth, childhood, sickness, and death. He is present at weddings and funerals. You can find the full range of human experience embodied in his teachings, which all point toward that greater imminent reality—the Kingdom of the Father.

Directly or indirectly, James would have heard about his brother's teachings. Simultaneously, James would be putting his energies into his own teachings and organizational efforts. How might his work and that of Jesus have been similar? How might they have been quite different?

How might James have felt as he receives word of his brother's becoming more and more popular? When word comes to him about someone being healed through Jesus' ministry, how might James have felt? Proud? "Yes, he's *my* brother!" Skeptical? "Now what is that brother of mine doing?" Or might he be somewhat torn and ambivalent in his feelings?

Apparently, James is not regularly among the disciples who travel with Jesus, but is simply a member of Jesus' family who is sometimes concerned and even embarrassed by him and his activities. In the Gospels, James is scarcely mentioned except on the occasion of having to deal with a situation when Jesus' activities seem to be getting out of hand (Mark 3:20–34). Some even think Jesus may be "out of his mind" (Mark 3:21, NRSV).

Picture the scene: Jesus is inside the house and his mother and brothers are outside, unable to get in because of the crowd. So they send in a messenger who says, "Your mother and your brothers and sisters are outside, asking for you." And Jesus replies, "Who are my mother and my brothers?" Now that is a strange question to ask. Jesus then turns his eyes toward the people who are sitting with him inside the house and says, "Here are my mother and my brothers! Whoever does the will of God is my brother and sister and mother" (Mark 3:32–35, NRSV).

What does Jesus really mean by this? Is he expanding the relationship beyond his own family and kin to include all who are living in relationship with God and following God's will? Or is he actually feeling rather estranged from his own immediate flesh and blood?

After hearing a remark like this, how might Jesus' family have felt? In particular, what might have been James' reaction? With what feelings might James have gone back to Jerusalem to continue his own work?

The story is the same in Mark, Matthew, Luke, and also in *The Gospel of the Ebionites*, where Jesus says: "'Who is my mother and who are my brethren?' And he stretches forth his hand toward his disciples and says, 'These are my brethren and mother and sisters, who do the will of my Father'" (Gospel of the Ebionites 5, SV).

Opposition to Jesus Intensifies

The teachings of Jesus that called for a primary allegiance to the Kingdom of the Father began to be seen as subversive by the Pharisees. Calling Jesus "crazy" was one attempt to discredit him. Another was to ask trick questions, such as the one about paying taxes to Caesar.

Some Pharisees and Herodians come to Jesus trying to trap him by asking: "'Teacher we know that you are sincere, and teach the way of God in accordance with truth, and show deference to no one; for you do not regard people with partiality. Tell us, then, what you think. Is it lawful to pay taxes to the emperor or not?'" (Matt. 22:16–17, NRSV).

Knowing their hypocrisy, Jesus says to them, "'Why are you putting me to the test, you hypocrites? Show me the coin used for the tax.' And they bring him one. Jesus says, 'Whose head is this, and whose title?' They answer, 'The emperor's.' Jesus says to them, 'Give therefore to the emperor the things that are the emperor's, and to God the things that are God's.'" (Matt. 22:18–21, NRSV).

And they are amazed at him. Jesus' saying resembles a Zen koan. The response Jesus gives seems to be an answer, but he leaves his listeners still trying to figure out what is the emperor's and what is God's! If all the earth belongs to the Lord, then what is Jesus really saying?

The Gospel of Thomas has another response that I find even more delightful: people show Jesus a gold coin and say, "'Caesar's men demand taxes from us.'" And Jesus replies, "'Give Caesar what belongs to Caesar, give God what belongs to God, *and give Me what is Mine!*'" (Gospel of Thomas 100, NHL, author's italics). With an answer like this, Jesus slips out of the trap and turns the problem back to his questioners, often infuriating them. As one might expect, opposition to Jesus escalates. According to the Gospels, there are various attempts to kill Jesus. After hearing Jesus teaching in his hometown, the people are so enraged that "they got up, drove him out of the town, and led him to the brow of the hill on which their town was built, so that they might hurl him off the cliff. But he passed through the midst of them and went on his way" (Luke 4:29–30, NRSV).

On another occasion, people "took up stones again to stone him." But Jesus seems to have talked his way out of that one. They try to arrest him instead, "but he escaped from their hands" (John 10:31, 39, NRSV).

Resistance to Jesus and his teachings increases until finally the established religious authorities use their influence to arrange for Jesus' trial, conviction, and execution. Apparently, from the stories, James was not a direct witness of his brother's death.

How Might James Have Dealt with His Brother's Death?

After the death of Jesus, how might James have felt? Can you imagine having a brother convicted as a criminal and publicly executed? There would be, of course, the personal feelings, plus the notoriety and word around town. What is life like for brothers of convicted felons?

It would have been quite unpleasant and even dangerous for anyone who had known Jesus, let alone a member of his family, to remain anywhere in the vicinity of Jerusalem.

In a purely practical way, wouldn't it have made much more sense for James to leave Jerusalem as soon as possible, head to Galilee, or even attempt to start his own life all over again as freshly as possible in a new location where no one knew him? Common sense might say to James, "Go somewhere else, get lost, start over, make a new life for yourself."

But nothing like that occurs. James is established in this city, has his contacts and his work. James chooses to remain in Jerusalem, the most volatile place possible, he associates with other courageous friends and followers of the late Jesus and finds himself thrust into a leadership position.

Being an opposition high priest, James has already been living with the very real possibility that his own life could be in danger. With the execution of his brother, Jesus, James' own future is in ever greater jeopardy.

In light of circumstances, James has some choices: Will he be more careful or go into hiding? Will he double his resolve and commit himself even more strongly to what he believes in?

James Experiences His Risen Brother

As James is sorting out what course of action to take, he experiences his risen brother. "Then he [the Resurrected Jesus] appeared to James, then to all the apostles" (1 Cor. 15:7, NRSV). I will relate two stories about James' experiences: one from the Gospel of the Hebrews and the other from the Apocalypse of James.

Although an extant copy of the Gospel of the Hebrews does not exist, we have brief quotations from it in the writings of Clement of Alexandria (ca. 150–215 C.E.), Origen (ca. 185–254 C.E.), Cyril, Bishop of Jerusalem (ca. 350 C.E.), and Jerome (ca. 400 C.E.).

It is Jerome who provides us with the Gospel of the Hebrews' story of one of James' experiences of the Resurrected Jesus:

> And when the Lord had given the linen cloth to the servant of the priest, he went to James and appeared to him. For James had sworn that he would not eat bread from that hour in which he had drunk the cup of the Lord until he should see him risen from among them that sleep. And shortly thereafter the Lord said: "Bring a table and bread!" He took the bread, blessed it and brake it and gave it to James the Just and said to him: "My brother, eat thy bread, for the Son of Man is risen from among them that sleep."[3]

What might it have been like for James to do something as simple as eating bread only to discover that his brother is alive and has something to say to him?

James is one of the first people to perceive the Resurrected Jesus through a simple meal. It is a common human experience for people to sense the presence of their loved ones who have died when those bereft are gathered for meals.

If someone you have lived with has died and you sit alone at the table where the two of you regularly ate together, you may very well experience first the loss of that person. Instead of a shared meal, you are eating alone; or if it is a family, all are gathered, but one is missing. You miss the person and feel the loss. The time may come when you sit down for the familiar meal and are aware that the loved one is now present with you. It is in the familiar that we find the Eternal.

The simple meal that James experienced evolved and has become a gathering that now goes by many names, including the Lord's Supper, the Eucharist, the Mass, the Holy Communion, the Liturgy, and the Holy Mysteries.

The theologies, expectations, and experiences of people in these rites vary considerably. Sometimes these rites may be little more than routine observances, whereas at other times they may bring a deep sense of the presence of the Resurrected Jesus.

Today we start with the rite and hope to have the experience but in the early days it was the other way around: first came the experience, then the rite!

First and Second Apocalypses of James

Another encounter of James with his risen brother is provided by *The First Apocalypse of James* and *The Second Apocalypse of James*. Neither of these appear in a conventional New Testament, but both are in the Nag Hammadi Library. These documents are written as conversations between James and the Risen Lord. Who wrote them? Where and when were they written? At this point, the research on these questions is inconclusive.

One thing is clear: these documents are not actual transcriptions of conversations between James and his risen brother. However, they are the authentic spiritual experiences of someone who found the figure of James a convenient peg on which to hang his or her teaching.

Literal truth and mythic truth weave in and out of each other and both provide us with living symbols through which we, too, can enter into deeper experiences of the Risen One who seeks to live within us.

Consider a few excerpts from conversations in the two Apocalypses of James: "It is the Lord who spoke with me: 'See now the completion of my redemption. I have given you a sign of these things, James, my brother'" (The First Apocalypse of James 24:10–18, NHL).

> James said, "Rabbi, if they arm themselves against you, then is there no blame?
>
> You have come with knowledge, that you might rebuke their forgetfulness.
>
> You have come with recollection, that you might rebuke their ignorance . . .
>
> You walked in mud, and your garments were not soiled, and you have not been buried in their filth, and you have not been caught."
> (First Apocalypse of James 28:5–20, NHL).

Through the Resurrected Jesus comes "knowledge that rebukes forgetfulness." A serious problem for many human beings is that they have forgotten who they are. Deep within each of us is the knowledge of who we really are, sons and daughters of the Source of Life who goes by many names: God, Father, the Eternal, the Name Beyond Names. The Resurrected Jesus seeks to awaken us to our true identity so that we might know with clarity who we are, not just conceptually, but experientially. Most, but not all, people know who their blood parents are; how many know their Eternal Parents? How many know that they are each a Child of the Universe?

The Resurrected Jesus comes with "recollection that rebukes ignorance," which is another way of saying the same thing. Recollect, remember, know that you are part of the Whole!

The following is an excerpt of a conversation between James and the Resurrected Jesus:

> And the Lord appeared to[James]. Then [James] stopped his prayer and embraced him. He kissed him, saying, "Rabbi, I have found you! . . ." [And the Lord said,] "Since you are a just man of God, you have embraced me and kissed me."
> (First Apocalypse of James 31:1–9, 32:6–9, NHL).

The kiss is more than a sign of affection or of intimacy. It is an expression of knowing the Eternal Wisdom, Sophia. Jesus was a historic male human being, but the Resurrected Jesus provides the complementarity needed for any human being, male or female. The kiss is that sign of connection and the symbol of the new life being conceived within us.

In another excerpt there is yet another kiss:

"And he kissed my mouth. He took hold of me, saying, 'My beloved! Behold, I shall reveal to you those things that neither the heavens nor their archons have known. . . . Behold, I shall reveal to you everything, my beloved.'"
(Second Apocalypse of James 56:15–20, 57:4–5 NHL).

What feelings might you have when you are open to receiving the kiss of the Resurrected Jesus? Some may have difficulty relating to this kind of resurrection experience. Others may know quite immediately what these stories are saying. Often those who understand are at a loss to find the right words to describe the feeling.

One of the most intimate of the resurrection stories is this one revealing the closeness between James and Jesus. This is a spiritual closeness and intimacy out of which comes new awareness for James, among them his view of women.

James said, ". . . Another thing I ask of you: who are the seven women who have been your disciples? And behold, all women bless you. I am also amazed how powerless vessels have become strong by a perception which is in them."
(First Apocalypse of James 38:15–23, NHL).

Men like James and countless other men have mistakenly seen women as "powerless vessels." But James recognizes that Jesus treats women as equals and serves as a catalyst putting them in touch with their inner potential. Does James gain a new understanding about women from this conversation?

When both men and women are experiencing more of what the Risen One offers, weakness turns into a new kind of strength. This does not mean power over another, but rather the strength of shared energy; competition is replaced with cooperation.

Recall what James' relationship with his brother Jesus might have been like and compare it with his new awareness given to him through the Resurrected Jesus. What might have been going on in James as he became aware that his dead brother has been resurrected?

I find it intriguing to imagine what his experience might have been like and what he might have gone through to resolve the conflicts that may have gone back so many years, even to those youthful days when he and Jesus were brothers playing and possibly fighting together.

I suspect that the change may have been transformative, like that of a caterpillar becoming a butterfly.

4

Thomas, Twin Brother of Jesus?

The classic resurrection story of Jesus and Thomas is found in John 20. The disciples are gathered in the house and experience the Resurrected Jesus, who stands among them and says, "Shalom!" which means, "Peace be with you." Then he shows them his hands and his side. The disciples rejoice when they see the Lord and Jesus says again, "Shalom! Peace be with you!" This time the Resurrected Jesus "breathes" on the disciples, saying, "Receive the Holy Spirit."

When the disciples gather, Thomas, the Twin, is missing. Where is he? Why has he gone off by himself? Whatever his reasons for being away, he soon returns to his friends, who attempt to express in words what they have experienced with the Resurrected Jesus. When Thomas hears what they have to say, he replies, "Unless I see the mark of the nails in his hands, and put my finger in the mark of the nails and my hand in his side, I will not believe" (John 20:25, NRSV).

As a result of making this response, he has been nicknamed "Doubting Thomas." For nearly two thousand years, Thomas has had the reputation of being "The Doubter," as though that was all that could be said about him. The assumption seems to be that one should believe without questioning. Yet the story itself reveals that when Thomas asks his questions, his curiosity is sparked, and he decides to remain with the others to see what might happen next. One week later when the Risen Lord returns, Thomas is present. He, too, becomes aware of the Resurrected Jesus and hears him say, "Put your finger here and see my hands. Reach out your hand and put it in my side. Do not doubt but believe." This time Thomas answers, "My Lord and my God" (John 20:27–28, NRSV).

How shall we understand this story? This resurrection story is from the Gospel of John, written about 90 C.E., approximately sixty years after the death of Jesus. How much is this Gospel recording historic events? How much might it be a meditative commentary on the rich meaning of the Jesus Event and, in particular, the Resurrected Jesus?

18

Which body are the disciples experiencing? Are they looking at the same body of Jesus that had been nailed to a cross? Many faith-filled people accept the story as literal historic fact. However, there are other ways of understanding and experiencing the meaning of the story, particularly through the symbols of the wounds in the hands and the side.

Just as Jesus is wounded, so Christ's risen body is wounded time and time again. Those who take seriously the Way that Jesus teaches run the same risks of both inner and outer wounding.

Meditation on the meaning of the wounds continues, and by the fourth century another writer, John Chrysostom, writes: "*There flowed from his side water and blood.* Beloved, do not pass over this mystery without thought; it has yet another hidden meaning, which I will explain to you. I said that water and blood symbolized baptism and the holy eucharist. From these two sacraments the Church is born."[1]

Clearly, John Chrysostom in the fourth century is providing us with a symbolic understanding of the story. Might the original writer of John at the end of the first century have also been doing the same thing?

How does one describe the indescribable? Language fails. Symbols convey the meaning and are designed to release in us the experiences known by those who knew them originally.

The Voice speaks to us and says, "Put your finger here and see my hands. Reach out your hand and put it in my side." Hearing this, how do we respond? Is a responsive chord struck in our hearts and souls? When we have "ears to hear," then we, too, will be able to say, "My Lord and my God!"

Once our hearts and souls have touched something of the Risen One living within us, then we face the same dilemma of the disciples and Thomas: How do we go about trying to relate to others what we have experienced? The best ways, of course, is to speak from experience and use our own words.

The Acts of Thomas

As we have seen, there are four sons of Mary. James is named first and Jesus is last. In between are two brothers, Simon and Judas Thomas, not to be confused with Judas Iscariot. The name Thomas comes from *thoma* in Aramaic, which means "twin." So is this third brother the twin of Jesus?

In the third century *Acts of Thomas*, 39, we find this colorful story[2]

While the apostle Thomas is standing in the highway and speaking with the crowd, an ass's colt comes, stands before him, opens its mouth and says, "Twin brother of Christ, apostle of the Most High and fellow initiate into the hidden word of Christ, who dost receive his secret sayings . . ."

This story follows in the tradition of talking animals, as in the story of Balaam's ass. Several times[3] during a journey, the ass sees an angel in the road and stops. Balaam is spiritually blind and does not see. Finally, Balaam and his ass have a conversation, and then Balaam becomes aware, sees the angel, and hears the message.

Startling stories like this disturb our ordinary sense of reality and ask us to say, "What in the world could this possibly mean?" Those who first heard the story of the ass's colt who speaks to Thomas would have already been familiar with the story of Balaam's ass. For them, a talking donkey is no problem; they are ready to hear what the donkey has to say!

The first-century *Gospel of Thomas* opens by saying, "These are the secret sayings which the living Jesus spoke and which Didymos Judas Thomas wrote down" (Gospel of Thomas, NHL). Curiously, Didymos means twin, and Thomas means twin so this Judas is the twin twin of Jesus!

What difference does this make for us? Most of us are accustomed to the idea of seeing Jesus as Brother to all of us. Meditate on that concept, and what it might mean.

What we see in these very old stories usually begins with a reflection of our own experience. Do you have one or more brothers? Or do you have a sister or two or more? If so, how would you describe your relationships with your sibling(s)? If you are an only child, do you feel that you missed out on something important in your life? Or were you happy to be the only one?

Think of brothers or sisters you know. How well do they get along with each other? Are there times when they provoke each other and fight with each other? Are there times when they have a special understanding of each other, learn from each other, and work well together?

The wide variety of relationships among brothers and sisters can provide a sense of what is possible for us with the Resurrected Jesus, who is available not only as a brother, but as our twin!

Twins Share Their Secrets

In The Book of Thomas the Contender (NHL), composed in Syria in the first half of the third century, we have a further development of the meaning of the Resurrected Jesus as twin.[3] The book opens with these lines:

"The secret words that the Savior spoke to Judas Thomas which I, even I Matthaias, wrote down—I was walking, listening to them speak with one another." Can you visualize the scene? The Resurrected Jesus and his brother Thomas are walking along together. Matthaias is tagging along behind, eavesdropping, and this is what he hears the Savior say:

"Brother Thomas, while you have time in the world, listen to me and I will reveal to you the things you have pondered in your mind" (Book of Thomas the Contender 138:1–4, NHL).

What a way to start a conversation! If someone were to open a conversation with you by saying, "I am going to tell you everything you have been wondering about," how might that feel to you? How would the other person know what you had been turning over in your mind? At the very least, such a statement would catch your attention.

There is an old saying that "when the student is ready, the teacher will appear." Whenever you enter into an experience with the Resurrected Jesus, you may very well discover fresh ways of looking at the very things that have been on your mind.

The Resurrected Jesus continues, "Now since it has been said that you are my twin and true companion, examine yourself that you may understand who you are, in what way you exist, and how you will come to be" (138:7–10, NHL). Think about this phrase, "examine yourself." The teaching, the information that you and I need can be discovered within ourselves!

Moreover, the Resurrected Jesus says, "Since you are called my brother, it is not fitting that you be ignorant of yourself" (138:10–12, NHL).

Notice the direction of this resurrection story: instead of being a better way of understanding Jesus, here is a better way of understanding ourselves!

The Resurrected Jesus continues, "And I know that you have understood, because you had already understood that I am the knowledge of the truth" (138:12–13, NHL).

Now the Resurrected Jesus moves more deeply into an understanding of this relationship: "So while you accompany me, although you are uncomprehending, you have (in fact) already come to know, and you will be called, 'the one who knows himself.' For he who has not known himself has known nothing, but he who has known himself has at the same time already achieved knowledge about the Depth of the All" (138:14–18).

This teaching of the Resurrected Jesus in the third century *Book of Thomas the Contender* in the Nag Hammadi Library matches rather well with the teachings of Jesus as recorded in the first-century *Gospel of Thomas:*

"If those who lead you say to you, 'See, the Kingdom is in the sky,' then the birds of the sky will precede you. If they say to you, 'It is in the sea,' then the fish will precede you. Rather, the Kingdom is inside of you, and it is outside of you. When you come to know yourselves, then you will become known, and you will realize that it is you who are the sons of the living Father.

(Gospel of Thomas 3, NHL)

Jesus continues his teaching with a warning for those who do not look within themselves.

"But if you will not know yourselves, you dwell in poverty and it is you who are that poverty" (Gospel of Thomas 3, NHL).

Might there be a price to pay for those who are unwilling to work toward knowing themselves?

Go deep enough into yourself, and what do you find? You find more than yourself: you find the deepest Self of All. Some call this the *Imago Dei*, the Image of God. After all, we are made in the image and reflection of God, are we not? Suppose we reach those deepest recesses of our souls and discover how true this is!

Jesus offers some very simple ways of discovering deep reality, as when he says, "The man old in days will not hesitate to ask a small child seven days old about the place of life, and he will live" (Gospel of Thomas 4, NHL). Have you ever tried that? Hold a tiny infant in your arms, look the child in the eye, and ask, "Little baby, is there something you have to teach me?" See what happens.

With this illustration, Jesus continues and says, "Recognize what is in your sight, and that which is hidden from you will become plain to you. For there is nothing hidden that will not become manifest" (Gospel of Thomas 5, NHL).

What might Jesus be getting at here? Could it be that when I do not know myself, the unconscious parts will still manifest themselves? Jung makes it clear that much of our behavior is the result of unconscious forces driving our actions. Unconscious actions can be quite destructive of ourselves and others. What Jung reminds us about, Jesus already knew, and the Resurrected Jesus repeats again and again. Possibly the most succinct statement of the Resurrected Jesus to us could be summarized in two words ascribed to Plato several centuries before the birth of Jesus: "Know thyself!"

5

Salome,
Sister of Jesus

According to the Gospels, Jesus had sisters (Mark 6:3; Matt. 13:56). How many sisters he may have had is an open question. Only Mark identifies one of the sisters by name, Salome.

The first time Mark mentions her is at the cross: "There were also women looking on from a distance; among them were Mary Magdalene, and Mary the mother of James the younger and of Joses, and Salome. These used to follow him and provided for him when he was in Galilee; and there were many other women who had come up with him to Jerusalem" (Mark 15:40–41, NRSV).

Salome is also there at the tomb on the first Easter morning: "When the sabbath was over, Mary Magdalene, and Mary the mother of James and Salome bought spices so that they might go and anoint him" (Mark 16:1, NRSV).

Imagine what this experience might be like for a sister of Jesus. Assuming she is younger than Jesus, she is probably a woman in her twenties who finds herself with her mother and her brother's closest woman companion, taking loving care of his battered body after a horrifying public execution by torture and crucifixion.

Today when someone dies, we call the funeral director, who comes quickly, takes the body away, and does what is needed. The next time we see the body of our family member, it is lying serenely in a casket. If there is cremation, we see nothing again except the urn of cremains.

But in the first century, the women are the ones responsible for caring for the dead. From womb to tomb, women are present bearing all the pains, all the joys, and everything else that life serves up. The women of the family care for the body themselves, washing it and then anointing it with traditional spices. Women are expected to be there, but when in the Gospels do we hear directly from them about their feelings?

With the possible exception of *The Gospel of Mary*, the records come to us from men, not the women themselves. Using our own active imagination, however, we may get a sense of what the experience of Salome might have been like "very early on the first day of the week" (Mark 16:2, NRSV).

23

She has been through pain and grief as a witness of the crucifixion. Now Jesus is dead, and she has the task with her mother and her brother's companion to bring spices to the tomb to anoint the body. What would it take emotionally to be able to do what must be done?

What may the women have been saying to each other as they walk along? Are they moving ahead with steady purpose or helping each other with faltering steps? What are they talking about? Are they discussing events of the last few days? Are they recalling scenes going back to years ago? Are they sometimes walking in silence? What thoughts might be in their minds? Are scenes from the past flashing into mind? Are they simply, quietly, purposefully moving toward what they know must be done?

Among the new data on Jesus is a small portion of *The Gospel of Peter* that a French archaeologist discovered in a monk's grave at Akhmim in Upper Egypt in 1886. Most of the *The Gospel of Peter* is still missing, but this small portion contains fascinating stories of Jesus' trial, crucifixion, and resurrection, including dialogue of the three women on their way toward the tomb.

> Although on the day he was crucified we could not weep and beat our breasts, we should not perform these rites at his tomb. But who will roll away the stone for us, the one placed at the entrance of the tomb, so that we may enter and sit beside him and do what ought to be done? We fear that someone might see us. And if we are unable to roll the stone away we should, at least, place at the entrance the memorial we have brought him, and we should weep and beat our breasts until we go home.
>
> (Gospel of Peter 12:3–5, SV)

The symbols in the story contain great meaning. Consider the stone: From the perspective of those approaching the tomb, what might it feel like to anticipate being blocked by a stone too big and heavy to move by themselves? What might it be like to be blocked from doing this last good thing for a loved one who has died?

In Mark's version of the story, the stone has already been rolled away. In Matthew's version there is an earthquake, and an angel of the Lord descends from heaven, rolls the stone away, and then sits on it.

In Mark, the women see a young man dressed in a white robe sitting on the right side of the tomb. In Matthew, there is an angel with appearance like lightning; he wears a robe that is white as snow. And in Luke's version, there are two men in "dazzling apparel" standing beside them.

Which is it: one man, one angel, or two men? Is this an angel, a man, or both? Angels are often messengers in human form, as in the story of the three men who visit Abraham and Sarah (Genesis 18).

Regarding the question of the other figures present, I find Luke's version of the story the one packed with the greatest symbolic meaning. Luke's Easter morning scene is based on the story of the transfiguration, where two men appear with Jesus on the mount and are identified as Moses and Elijah. In Luke's story of the ascension, again there are two men. So the theme carries through all three stories—transfiguration, resurrection, and ascension—with the same pair, Moses and Elijah, in all three.

The Gospel of Peter expands on this theme even further by saying that it is during the night preceding that the heavens are torn open, the two men come down in a burst of light, and the stone rolls away by itself. The two men enter the tomb. Next the two men come out of the tomb with a third! So Moses and Elijah have come to get Jesus; together all three go up into the heavens. Only the Roman soldiers are witness to this scene: "They see three men leaving the tomb, two supporting the third, and a cross was following them. The heads of the two reached up to the sky, while the head of the third, whom they led by the hand, reached beyond the skies. And they heard a voice from the skies that said, 'Have you preached to those who sleep?' and an answer was heard from the cross: 'Yes!'" (Gospel of Peter 10:2–5, SV).

The Gospel of Peter is the only Gospel that provides a story of the body of Jesus leaving the tomb. This is a "night before" story. All the other Gospels start with the "morning after." There has been a brilliance during the night. The women are experiencing the afterglow in the morning.

One or two of the men return to cue the women. In the Gospel of Mark, they stand by the women with this message: "Do not be alarmed; you are looking for Jesus of Nazareth, who was crucified. He has been raised; he is not here. Look, there is the place where they laid him" (Mark 16:6, NRSV).

In the Gospel of Luke the message is in the form of a direct question, "Why do you look for the living among the dead?" (Luke 24:5, NRSV).

What would it feel like for Salome to go to the tomb with the other women and find that the body is gone? They do not know that Moses and Elijah have come for him during the night.

A missing person can cause anxiety. But to know with certainty that your brother is dead and then to discover his body missing could be especially disconcerting!

Before Salome and the other women can adjust to Jesus' absence, there is a clear message to them from the messenger: "Go, tell his disciples and Peter that he is going ahead of you to Galilee; there you will see him, just as he told you" (Mark 16:7, NRSV).

Galilee is the region where Jesus has spent the greater part of his ministry of teaching and healing. The message is simple and direct: "Go to the familiar places where you were with him before, and there you will see him." After someone has died, those who remain will often speak of feeling the presence of the beloved departed when they revisit the places where ordinary life experiences occurred in the past. When someone dies, the absence is felt very deeply and poignantly, and then comes the surprise of resurrection: the beloved lives within those who remain. Salome, her mother Mary, and Mary Magdalene have heard the message to go to Galilee, and so there is no need to remain around the tomb. They go out and "flee" from the tomb with two simultaneous emotions—"terror and amazement" (Mark 16:8, NRSV).

Willis Barnstone's translation says they were "seized by trembling and ecstasy." Barnstone adds this footnote: "The earliest manuscripts end with the dramatic fear of the women in *ekstasis*, here rendered 'ecstasy,' which conveys the literal meaning of 'being outside themselves' as well as 'ecstasy' with its multiple meanings of 'amazement' in 'being elsewhere' and "beside themselves" with fear."[1]

In Salome's experience, her brother is gone and his body is nowhere to be seen. She runs with fear and ecstasy. Today, with the practice of cremation increasing, the body is quickly "gone." Whatever remains of our brother or sister or parent or loved one is to be discovered in our own "Galilees," the familiar places shared before the person's death.

When a brother or friend dies, does the relationship end? You can no longer see your brother as you did before or do the things you did together before. But like Salome, Mary Magdalene, and the other women, you can go to the tomb and find that he is not there. Not there? Where have they taken him? But our anguish is followed by another deeper reality; he has risen from the dead and is still alive in us!

Once we experience and know the reality of resurrection, then we are ready to discover how to go through the separations we experience with relatives and friends—not only those who die, but also those who move away, those who turn away, those who for whatever reason seem not to be present to us as before.

But there is an abiding truth: whatever two people give to one another remains and cannot go away or disappear because it continues to reside in the depths of their souls. Once upon a time I made a most amazing discovery. I realized I had stepped into Eternal Time where all my family, friends, lovers, teachers, and opponents live. Those who have died and those with whom I have lost touch are within me. Even my best friend in high school who refuses to talk to me because he thinks I have departed from the faith, remains with me. All whom I have known are lodged in the deep recesses of my soul.

6

Mourners Gathering
in the Family Home

After someone dies, the rest of the family gathers somewhere, usually in the family home. For the family of Jesus, where might that be? At first glance, there appears to be no specific mention of a family home in any of the documents that have come down to us. However, there is a reference to the disciples gathering in Jerusalem in the home of "Mary, the mother of John whose other name was Mark" (Acts 12:12, NRSV).

At first reading this would seem to be yet another Mary. Incidentally, we have not heard of her before, and we do not hear of her again. So who is she, really?

By the time the Acts of the Apostles is written, the virgin birth story has been introduced in the Gospel of Luke, the companion volume to Acts. One very real possibility is that the stories of the mythic Mary are now taking over the place of the historic Mary. The result is that she seems to vanish from the story, which would be very unusual for a character as important as the mother of Jesus.

Maybe it is time for us to try reading between the lines and to look carefully for those places where Mary, mother of Jesus, may be present in disguise. Might it be possible that this Mary in whose home people are gathering is Mary, mother of James and Jesus and their siblings?

Another possibility is that family and friends are gathering in the home of James, who is already established in Jerusalem. "When the day of Pentecost had come, they were all together in one place" (Acts 2:1, NRSV). The "place" may very well be James' home, Mary's home, or somewhere else.

> When they [120 people] had entered the city, they went to the room upstairs where they were staying, Peter, and John, and James, and Andrew, Philip and Thomas, Bartholomew and Matthew, James son of Alphaeus, and Simon the Zealot, and Judas son of James. All these were constantly devoting themselves to prayer, together with certain women, including Mary the mother of Jesus, as well as his brothers"
> (Acts 1:13–14, NRSV).

27

So unless any of these went off somewhere, it would seem safe to assume that all of the above were present on the day of Pentecost. Jesus' mother and his brothers, James, Simon, and Judas Thomas, would have been there, plus "certain women." How I wish the writer had given us their names! This leaves us having to make some educated guesses. If all were gathering in this place to share their grief and be family to one another, then surely the women present would be Salome and the other sisters of Jesus, Mary Magdalene, Joanna, and possibly Suzanna. Surely they would be present with the rest of the family and friends during the time of mourning.

What normally happens when friends and family gather in a home after someone dies? It all depends upon the family and the culture, of course. I've seen the sexes separating, with the women gathering in the kitchen and the men in the living room or out on the porch. That is just one scenario, but I cite it to raise the question: Do you envision the mourners of Jesus gathering all together or with the men in one place and the women in another?

From the way the story is told, the scene could have taken place either way. Because they were "all together" in one place, it could be seen as one group of men and women. On the other hand, because the women are scarcely mentioned except as "certain women," maybe they were apart from the men.

Temple worship at that time would have had men and women separated. However, Jesus had women as well as men traveling with him, so he was bringing a fresh sense of equality. In his death, do you see his egalitarian principle prevailing? Or do you imagine a quick return to the old tradition of keeping the sexes apart?

Together or separately, we are told they are praying. Can you hear them? Is this silent meditation or loud wailing? Are they singing familiar psalms that give expression to their feelings, or are they saying whatever comes from their hearts?

Have you been to gatherings of mourners and funerals where people are either not saying very much or talking about everything except what has happened? How much are people here in this scene expressing their grief? How much is their grief still hidden?

In the Gospel writer's chronology, the mourners have been gathering from Passover until Pentecost,[1] in other words, for seven weeks. If the time frame is extended like this, then their conversations might have included feelings like pain in losing Jesus, anger toward the authorities, and fear of what might happen next. Who will lead them now?

Curiously, the Acts of the Apostles has a story of the election of someone to take the place of Judas Iscariot and bring the number of apostles from eleven back up to twelve. Is having exactly twelve really that important? Why is there no mention of choosing a new leader now that Jesus is gone? Later in the story we discover that James has become the leader of the Jerusalem assembly, but there is no account of how this happened. Apparently, the story of electing Matthias to take the place of Judas Iscariot has been created and put into the narrative where the selection of James as leader would otherwise belong.[2]

James is already a leader in Jerusalem and has his own following. James is Jesus' brother, probably the eldest. There is a strong Middle Eastern tradition that when one brother dies another steps forward to take his place. James is thrust into leadership for the followers of his brother as well as his own followers. He has the monumental task of bringing both groups together.

Rushing Wind and Fire

The event that energizes this assembly is Pentecost, a story told very succinctly but with symbols that are powerful beyond the imagination:

> When the day of Pentecost had come, they were all together in one place. And suddenly from heaven there came a sound like the rush of a violent wind, and it filled the entire house where they were sitting. Divided tongues, as of fire, appeared among them, and a tongue rested on each of them. All of them were filled with the Holy Spirit and began to speak in other languages, as the Spirit gave them ability (Acts 2:1–4, NRSV).

Start with the "sound like the rush of a violent wind." The sound is not outside threatening the house but is swirling around inside! What might that feel like? Would it be energy originating inside and moving out? Symbols attempt to convey the feeling of the people. Each person in the group, and the entire group, is feeling tremendous power.

Now add tongues of fire, leaping and licking everything in sight. Fire takes one substance like wood and transforms its energy into light, heat, and ashes. Hence, fire is a symbol of transformation.

What kind of transformation is occurring here for the mourners in the family home on Pentecost? Might it be that all the shattered hopes, painful grief, intense anger, and gripping fear are being transformed into something new? The story goes on to say that "all of them were filled with the Holy Spirit and began to speak in other languages, as the Spirit gave them ability." Clearly, this is the power of the Holy Spirit set loose inside the house and, more important, inside the people who are gathered.

The Pentecost story begins with the family, friends, and followers of Jesus and then spreads like wildfire.

Now there were devout Jews from every nation under heaven living in Jerusalem. And at this sound the crowd gathered and was bewildered, because each one heard them speaking in the native language of each. Amazed and astonished, they asked, "Are not all these who are speaking Galileans? And how is it that we hear, each of us, in our own native language?"

(Acts of the Apostles 2:5–8, NRSV).

The sound is being heard outside the house, and the effects are quite astonishing: people are hearing and understanding one another! The list of people that follows includes people from all over the Mediterranean world.

"Parthians, Medes, Elamites, and residents of Mesopotamia, Judea and Cappodocia, Pontus and Asia, Phrygia and Pamphylia, Egypt and the parts of Libya belonging to Cyrene, and visitors from Rome, both Jews and proselytes, Cretans and Arabs—in our own languages we hear them speaking about God's deeds of power

(Acts of the Apostles 2:9–11, NRSV).

Remember the story of the Tower of Babel? A unified people with a common language start a building project, but their pride alienates them from God and one another. By the end of the story they are divided, speaking different languages without any understanding of one another. Pentecost reverses Babel. People who were divided are transformed by the power of the Holy Spirit, whose energy unites them in love and understanding.

Separated individuals are becoming members of one Body. They are experiencing the Resurrected Jesus in one another. What shall they call this new unity they are feeling? Before long they find the right words and give the experience a name: this is the Body of Christ.

7

Mother Earth
Shaking and Quaking

In one of his more startling sets of teachings, Jesus says, "Whoever does not hate his father and his mother as I do cannot become a disciple to Me. And whoever does not love his father and his mother as I do cannot become a disciple to Me. For my mother gave me falsehood, but My true Mother gave me life" (Thomas 101, NHL).

Who is Jesus' "true Mother"? Might Jesus be referring to the companion of God the Father? Wisdom (Sophia), who is one with the Lord from the beginning, says so clearly:

> When he established the heavens, I was there,
> when he drew a circle on the face of the deep,
> when he assigned to the sea its limit,
> so that the waters might not transgress his command,
> when he marked out the foundations of the Earth,
> then I was beside him, like a master worker;
> and I was daily his delight,
> rejoicing before him always.
>
> (Prov. 8:27–30, NRSV)

> I was with Him as a confidant,
> A source of delight every day.
>
> (Prov. 8:30, Tanakh)

Might Jesus be drawing on the Wisdom tradition within Judaism? Might God be both Mother and Father for Jesus? In light of Jesus' sense of connection with all of life and the many nature parables in his teaching, might he also be referring to Mother Earth as his "true Mother"?

According to the story, when Jesus was crucified he cried, "My God, my God, why have you forsaken me?" (Mark 15:34, NRSV). Where was his Father? Why was his Father silent?

31

And where was his divine Mother? Was she undisturbed? Or was she very powerfully moved by his death? According to *The Gospel of Peter*, when they pulled the nails from the Lord's hands and set Jesus' body on the ground, the whole Earth shook and there was great fear (Gospel of Peter 6:1, SV). Mother Earth feels human violence and does not take it lying down. At the death of Jesus she quakes! If the Father was absent, Mother Earth was very present.

The geology of Jerusalem reveals that it lies in a fault zone. It runs from the Rift Valley of Africa up through the southern end of the Dead Sea, underneath the Jordan River Valley, into the Sea of Galilee and on north. There is also a fault line running between the Mount of Olives and the city of Jerusalem. Connecting lines run just outside Jerusalem, where the crucifixion occurred.

This area has a long history of earthquakes. For example, the prophet Jeremiah in the seventh century B.C.E. observed, "I looked on the mountains, and lo, they were quaking, and all the hills moved to and fro" (Jer. 4:24, NRSV). Zechariah is even more explicit when he describes the coming of the day of the Lord. "On that day [the LORD'S] feet shall stand on the Mount of Olives, which lies before Jerusalem on the east; and the Mount of Olives shall be split in two from east to west by a very wide valley, so that one half of the Mount shall withdraw northward, and the other half southward" (Zech. 14:4, NRSV). This description matches precisely how fault lines function as one plate moves past the other, creating a tremendous jolt and aftershocks in the process.

The Gospel of Peter says the Earth quaked at the crucifixion. Given the geology of the area, it would have been perfectly possible for an Earthquake to have occurred during the Passion and death of Jesus.

Even more powerful than a literal quake is the symbolic message that when the body of Jesus touches the ground, the Earth moves! At the mythic level, these quakes are another way in which the Gospel writers are announcing that the Day of the Lord has dawned. A new age has begun.

The crucifixion isn't the first time that Mother Earth reacted to violence perpetrated upon her by human beings. In the Creation myths is the story of the first murder: Cain kills his brother Abel. Then the Lord comes into the Garden and asks, "Where is your brother Abel?" Cain replies, "I do not know; am I my brother's keeper?" (Gen. 4:10–11, NRSV).

The Lord poses an even deeper question, "What have you done? your brother's blood is crying out to me from the ground. And now you are cursed from the ground which has opened its mouth to receive your brother's blood from your hand" (Gen. 4:10–11, NRSV).

The message is clear: you cannot hide what you have done from the Blood, the Life Force, or the Holy Ground Herself! Mother Earth opens her mouth to receive the blood of Abel, and the blood cries out as it is being swallowed.

Throughout the ages, when human beings feel the ground moving under their feet they instinctively ask, "O my God, what have we done?" Today we have knowledge of plate tectonics and understand that the pressures from within the Earth are driving the plates and causing not only earthquakes, but volcanic action as well. As a result, we are often quick to dismiss as superstition the idea that human behavior has "caused" the Earth to move.

However, we are rediscovering that the Earth herself is one living organism with everything connected; human behavior does affect what happens on the Earth. For example, ecological study reveals the ways in which Nature reacts to deforestation and destruction of the rain forests, causing pollution of lakes, streams, rivers, and even the sea. The unrelenting ways in which we continue to rape and pillage her have disastrous results, including change of weather patterns and flooding. Mother Earth does not take destructive human actions lying down. She reacts.

There may be no direct causal connection between the violent behavior of human beings and the quaking of the Earth. But at the mythic level it is absolutely true that the Earth shakes when the broken, dead body of Jesus touches her. Blood will cry out from the ground, and the Earth herself shakes when human beings are violent toward one another and toward her.

On that first Easter morning as the women are moving toward the tomb, there is an angel and a violent earthquake (Matt 28:2). Jesus has risen, and the Earth moves and rejoices! Not only does she shake when she is upset and sad, but also when she is happy and joyous! Mother Earth is a very expressive woman: she knows how to wail and she knows how to celebrate!

Speaking of mother, Jesus is quoted as saying peculiar things about her: "My mother gave me falsehood, but My true Mother gave me life" (Gospel of Thomas 101, NHL). Who is this "mother"? Is she Mary, who gave birth to him, raised him, loved and nurtured him? If so, isn't he being a bit ungrateful? Or is Jesus referring to mother Jerusalem who has wandered from the truth and given him falsehood? What might Jesus really mean about falsehood coming from his mother?

Who is this "true Mother" who gives him life? During his baptism, Jesus feels very related to That Which IS, to the Source of all life; in feeling so connected Jesus says, "Abba, Father!" Might he also be acknowledging the Source of Life as Mother? How connected might Jesus have felt toward the Earth? Might she be the true Mother who gives Jesus life?

When does Jesus experience his true Mother? Does he see her when he is looking at the natural world around him? Does he hear her voice in the sounds of wind and birds? Might he also have discovered that his true Mother lives in the depths of his own soul?

The Earth quaked when Jesus died and again when Jesus rose from the dead. I suspect that many other times during his lifetime, Jesus felt her moving. She does her part by being expressive, and Jesus does his part by paying attention.

In the stories of Jesus' life, death, and resurrection, symbols like earthquakes increase our ecological awareness and deepen our spiritual understanding.

8

Peter,
Close Friend of Jesus

Peter is one of the first men to hear the invitation from Jesus to become his friend and disciple. He is the fisherman who literally drops his nets, leaves his work, and goes with Jesus throughout Galilee. He even provides a "base of operations" in his home in Capernaum, a place to which Jesus and the disciples can return and refresh themselves before going on yet another trip of teaching and healing.

Peter knows firsthand both the wide acceptance of the populace as well as the building resistance and opposition of the religious authorities. Peter is very much aware of the fact that the center of the opposition is in Jerusalem, so he is very surprised when Jesus announces his intention to go into the city.

Knowing that there is likely to be trouble, Peter "rebukes," or "lectures," Jesus. And Jesus "rebukes," or "reprimands," Peter. The tension between them is intense and builds to the point where Jesus says to Peter, "Get out of my sight, you Satan, you, because you're not thinking in God's terms, but in human terms" (Mark 8:33, NRSV and SV).

Hearing Jesus call him "Satan" must have left Peter reeling. All he is trying to do is keep Jesus from going into the city where there could be a good deal of trouble; Jesus might even lose his life. Who can blame Peter for wanting to protect Jesus from the inevitable consequences? I hear Peter saying to Jesus, "Stay up here in Galilee and do your teaching where it is safer. It is much too risky for you to go into the city, and we need you here! I am only saying this for your own good!"

But Jesus doesn't take Peter's advice. The argument is settled by Jesus, "who sets his face" toward Jerusalem as he has done on previous occasions when the danger was not so great. Jesus' determination to resist Peter's temptation is reminiscent of his encounter with Satan in the wilderness and the result of choosing the better way, even when it is difficult and risky to the point of death.

"Setting his face" is reminiscent of the prophet Second Isaiah, who "sets his face like flint" because he is convinced he will "not be put to shame" and that the One who "vindicates him is near" (Isaiah 50:7, NRSV). Second Isaiah asks questions that might very well have been roiling around in Jesus as well, "Who will contend with me? Let us stand up together. Who are my adversaries? Let them confront me. It is the Lord GOD who helps me; who will declare me guilty?" (Isaiah 50:8–9, NRSV).

Peter loses the argument and is unable to convince Jesus to be cautious. Jesus goes into Jerusalem and tensions build. At supper one evening, Jesus says, "Truly I tell you, one of you will betray me" (Mark 14:18, NRSV). Or in a more dramatic translation, "So help me, one of you eating with me is going to turn me in!" (SV).

The disciples are upset and asking, "I'm not the one, am I?" Next Jesus says to them, "You will all lose faith. . . ." And Peter states with great conviction, "Even if everyone else loses faith, I won't." Peter hears Jesus saying to him, "So help me, tonight before the rooster crows twice you will disown me three times" (Mark 14: 18, 19, 27, 29, 30, SV).

Events move quickly: a final testing in the Garden of Gethsemane, arrest followed by trials all night long. Most of the disciples scatter, but Peter loiters in the courtyard waiting for results.

A slave woman notices Peter and says to him, "You too were with that Nazarene, Jesus!" But Peter denies it, saying, "I haven't the slightest idea what you're talking about!"

The slave woman persists and tells others standing by, "This fellow is one of them!" but Peter denies it. A little later others say to Peter, "You really are one of them, since you also are a Galilean!" A Galilean accent and a Judean accent are like northern and southern accents in this country, very hard to disguise. At this point Peter begins to curse and swear, saying, "I don't know what you are talking about."

The trial has been going on all night, and then a rooster's call announces the dawn. On the second cock's crow, Peter remembers what Jesus has told him, "Before a rooster crows twice you will disown me three times!" And he breaks down and starts to cry (Mark 14:66–72, SV).

Can we even begin to imagine the mixed emotions Peter may have felt? After all, he had warned Jesus, so this time it's not Peter's fault. Peter risks arrest by remaining in the yard outside the courtroom so he can learn the verdict as soon as it is handed down. There are deep challenges to his friendship with Jesus.

Peter doesn't witness Jesus' torture and crucifixion. He and the other male disciples have made themselves scarce. Only Mary Magdalene, Jesus' mother, his sister Salome, and possibly a few other women have enough love, loyalty, and courage to stand nearby as Jesus is nailed to a cross and hangs there suffering and dying.

The women are the last to see Jesus alive and the first to experience the Resurrected Jesus. A bit later, Peter has his own experience of the Resurrected Jesus. The scene is set in a passage from *The Gospel of Peter*.

> Now it was the last day of Unleavened Bread, and many began to return to their homes since the feast was over. But we, the twelve disciples of the Lord, continued to weep and mourn, and each one, still grieving on account of what had happened, left for his own home. But I, Simon Peter, and Andrew, my brother, took our fishing nets and went away to the sea. And with us was Levi, the son of Alphaeus, whom the Lord . . .
>
> (Gospel of Peter 14:1–3, SV).

In *The Gospel of Peter* the story breaks off here, but it continues with full force in John 21. Quotations that follow are from the Scholars Version.

After the crucifixion, Peter has already said, "I'm going to go fishing." Jesus is dead, Peter's hopes are dashed, everything is over, so he might as well go back to what he knows—the fishing business. It might mean facing his fishermen friends and their taunts.

At the tomb are the Messengers who tell the women that they should go to Galilee, the familiar place, and there they will see Jesus, just as he has promised. The familiar place for Peter, of course, is down at the water doing what he knows best. Peter and his friends work all night, as before, and catch nothing at all. At daybreak the Risen Jesus is there on the shore, but Peter and the others "didn't recognize it was Jesus." Typical of resurrection appearances is the initial nonrecognition of the Resurrected Jesus by the family and friends of Jesus.

The Resurrected Jesus, who is not recognized at first, says to Peter, "You haven't caught any fish, have you?" Peter and the others reply, "No." Then he says, "Cast your net on the right side of the boat and you'll have better luck!"

Whatever Peter and the others are feeling, they take the suggestion and cast the nets once more. This time the catch is so good that they cannot haul in the huge number of fish that have been caught.

Then the "disciple whom Jesus loved most" says, "It is the Master!" Peter, hearing the word, ties his cloak around him, since he was stripped for work, and throws himself into the water. The rest of the men come in the boat, dragging the net full of fish. When they get back to shore, they see a charcoal fire burning with fish cooking on it and some bread.

Peter and the others hear a voice calling to them, "Bring some of the fish you've just caught. . . . Come and have breakfast!" None of the disciples dare to ask, "Who are you?" They know it is the Master. When they reach the shore, the Master takes bread and gives it to them and passes the fish around as well.

The power of the original stories about being "fishers of people" and the stories of feeding thousands with bread and fish now expand in this scene with new details added. When Peter and the others sit down and examine the catch, they find they have caught 153 fish in the net. Did anyone take time to count?

In the first century, the fisher folk had observed the various kinds of fish that were available to them in nearby lakes and in the Mediterranean Sea. They believed that there were exactly 153 kinds of fish in the world. But the literal number of varieties of fish is not the point. When we recognize 153 as a symbolic number representing all kinds of fish and realize that fish are symbols of people, then the message becomes clear: the net is gathering all kinds of people: no one is excluded or counted out. The implications of this symbol are far-reaching for our time. All people are to be included: infants, children, adults, the beloved dead; all races, nationalities, classes, and levels of intelligence; all sexual orientations.

The Persistent Question: "Do You Love Me?"

The next section of John 21 is focused specifically on Simon Peter. Just as he denied knowing Jesus three times, now he hears a persistent question, "Simon, John's son, do you love me more than they do?" After hearing the question the first time, Peter replies, "Of course, Master; you know I love you." Next Peter hears, "Then keep feeding my lambs." In other words, do something about it: show me you love me by the way you behave, by the action you take.

A second time Peter hears the question, "Simon, John's son, do you love me?" And again Peter replies, "Yes, Master, you know I love you." And then Peter hears, "Keep shepherding my sheep."

A third time Peter hears the question, "Simon, John's son, do you love me?" Peter is hurt that he is asked a third time, "Do you love me?"

Hearing the question the third time, Peter replies, "Master, you know everything; you know I love you."

"Keep feeding my sheep."

Peter's three denials of Jesus are matched with the persistent question from the Resurrected Jesus, "Do you love me?" When the one we have offended keeps asking us whether we still love him or her, and we know that we do, it can be irritating, especially when the number of askings parallels the number of hurts we have inflicted.

What happens for us when a loved one dies, especially if we have some unfinished business with that person? What happens when we have spoken as honestly as we could, have warned someone about impending disaster, and that person has not taken our advice and pushed on ahead? What happens when what we feared happens and worse? How do we deal with our denials, betrayals, and any other unresolved feelings?

When someone we love dies, we can expect to have persistent questions haunt us. They can be phrased in so many ways, but essentially they boil down to this basic one: "Do you love me?"

When someone dies, is there any way to become reconciled with that person? The strength of this and other resurrection stories is that our beloved dead continue through the pain and separation of death. They come alive in us. And, most amazing, the reconciliation that may have been lacking when they were living can be resolved within us after they die.

This resurrection story with Peter concludes with a rather unusual twist: Simon Peter hears these words spoken to him, "I swear to God, when you were young you used to gather your cloak around you and go where you wanted to go. But when you've grown old, you'll stretch out your arms, and someone else will get you ready and take you where you don't want to go" (John 21:18, SV). What might be the meaning of this additional message to Peter?

John's Gospel was written about sixty years after the death of Jesus. It contains less historical information and more meditative commentary on the events surrounding Jesus—his life, death, and resurrection. It includes traditions on the lives of Peter and others close to Jesus as well.

The theme of Peter "gathering his cloak around him" is one that has very deep roots, going back to the Creation story where Adam and Eve, who had been content to be naked in the Garden, suddenly felt the need to "cover themselves" when they were feeling guilty.

Peter, hearing the voice of the Master calling from the shore, felt he had to grab his cloak and cover up before jumping into the water, which is just the exact opposite of what would be expected: why get dressed and then go swimming? When we remember that this startling detail is there for a purpose, then it begins to make sense. If Peter is feeling guilty and ashamed for having denied Jesus in his hour of greatest need, then if this same one has returned, is it no wonder that Peter might want to cover himself?

Jesus in his teachings says, "When you disrobe without being ashamed and take up your garments and place them under your feet like little children and tread on them, then will you see the Son of the Living One, and you will not be afraid" (Gospel of Thomas 37, NHL).

If we have gained the wisdom of children, we may feel less need to cover up, less ashamed, more open, a greater ability to be ourselves, whatever that may entail. It is my conviction that Peter's experiences with the historic Jesus and with the Resurrected Jesus have enormous implications for our lives, particularly as we give loving attention to our relationships with the living and with our beloved departed—yes, with our own grateful dead.

9

Mary Magdalene and Teachings
from the Resurrected Jesus

Mary Magdalene's experience with the Resurrected Jesus in the Garden was just the beginning. New evidence of her ongoing experiences is provided in recently discovered and translated documents, most notably in the Gospel named in her honor.

The Gospel of Mary is likely to have originated in Syria in the late first or early second century. The good news is that we now have a significant portion of *The Gospel of Mary*, a document springing entirely from encounters with the Resurrected Jesus. The bad news is that the first six chapters are missing. We have to jump right into the middle of the story, where the Resurrected Jesus is in conversation with Mary Magdalene, Peter, Andrew, and Levi.

The Blessed One greets them all and says, "Peace be with you! Acquire my peace within yourselves! Be on your guard so that no one deceives you, 'Look over here!' or 'Look over there!' For the seed of the true humanity exists within you. Follow it! Those who search for it will find it" (Gospel of Mary 4:1–6, SV).

One of the most exciting discoveries in *The Gospel of Mary* is finding that the "seed of the true humanity" is the very heart of the gospel. The good news is that we can find our true selves and become more fully authentic human beings.

"Seed of the true humanity" is the same phrase as the one most often translated in the Gospels as "The Son of Man." The concept rests at the very heart and core of Jesus' own identity and teaching. Yet when it is translated in the gender specific terms "Son" and "Man," it is a double turnoff for many people. Karen L. King of Harvard Divinity School provides us with the fresh English translation, "seed of the true humanity."

I find it particularly exciting that it is through Mary Magdalene, the first person to experience the Resurrected Jesus, that the central teaching of Jesus is continued after his death. Why is it that a woman was the first to understand what Jesus meant? Why is it that translations made primarily by men have obscured the meaning for almost two thousand years? And why is it that a woman scholar is the first to render the phrase in a way accessible to all human beings?

To begin to understand the depth of meaning contained in this phrase, we might return to the teachings of Jesus in the Gospels of Mark, Matthew, Luke, and John, looking for the "Son of Man" phrase and substituting "Seed of True Humanity." Then those passages may come alive freshly for us and touch the living seed of our own potential that lives inside each human being. For a fuller discussion of "Son of Man: Seed of True Humanity," consult Appendix B at the back of this book.

After stating clearly that "the seed of the true humanity is within you," the Resurrected Jesus adds, "Go then and preach the good news. . . . Do not lay down any rule beyond what I ordained for you, nor promulgate law like the lawgiver, or else it will dominate you" (Gospel of Mary 4:8–10, SV).

After he said these things, the Blessed One left them. In other words, "Go tell others the good news about how to become authentic human beings. Tell them that the seed of the true humanity is already within them. Tell others everything you have learned from Jesus about how to experience and live this new life!"

One might expect great joy from the disciples in discovering that the teachings of Jesus about the authentic human being are alive and well, ready to be disseminated by them. But this instruction to carry on the teachings of Jesus carries a tremendous responsibility and involves enormous risk.

The Gospel of Mary tells us that the disciples were grieved and wept greatly, saying, "How are we going to go out to the rest of the world to preach the good news about the domain of the seed of true humanity?" (Gospel of Mary 5:2, SV). Then comes their real concern and fear: "If they did not spare him, how will they spare us?" (Gospel of Mary 5:3, SV).

What a paradox this is! Surely we human beings would like to discover how to live life most fully, so what is the risk? All our standard operating procedures, our self-identities, our values, everything about us is going to be challenged; in a word, we have to change.

Individually and collectively, we human beings usually resist change. If the disciples are expected to be agents of change by promoting this new gospel, then they have every right to expect that there will be resistance, opposition to the message, and great risk to themselves. Once again, "If they did not spare him, how will they spare us?"

Then Mary stands up. She greets them all and addresses her brothers, saying, "Do not weep and be distressed, nor let your hearts be irresolute. For his grace will be with you all and will shelter you. Rather, we should praise his greatness, for he has joined us together and made us true human beings. As Mary says these things, she turns their minds toward the Good and they begin to ask about the words of the Savior" (Gospel of Mary 5:4–8, SV).

Where did Mary get the strength to say these things with such assurance? Remember, she has gone through her own time of grieving and weeping in the

Garden and has already experienced the depths of her own distress. Mary changes when she experiences the Resurrected Jesus calling her by name.

Being the first person to experience the Resurrected Jesus and knowing what it is to have the risen life activated within her, she has a renewed heart. She knows from experience that Christ's grace is with her and is sheltering her.

What might it be like for her to feel sheltered? In a very real sense she is in Jesus and Jesus is in her. She is living the resurrected life that gives her gentle courage. She speaks to the other disciples what she knows from within her own heart.

Peter says to Mary, "Sister, we know that the Savior loved you more than any other woman. Tell us the words of the Savior that you know, but which we haven't heard." Mary responds, "I will report to you as much as I remember that you don't know." And she begins speaking these words to them. She says, "I saw the Lord in a vision and I said to him, 'Lord, I saw you today in a vision.' He said to me, "Congratulations to you for not wavering at seeing me. For where the mind is there is the treasure"\(Gospel of Mary 6:1–7:4, SV).

Whatever absorbs most of our mental energies reveals our greatest concerns and values. What do we think about most? Is this really our greatest treasure? Might there be something more valuable on which to focus our thinking?

Mary encounters the Resurrected Jesus in the visions of her heart and then asks this question, "Lord, how does a person who sees a vision see it—with the soul or with the spirit?" The Savior answers, "The visionary does not see with the soul or with the spirit, but with the mind which exists between these two— that is what sees the vision and that is what. . . ." (Gospel of Mary 7:5–6, SV).

At this point there is an abrupt break in the conversation. Four pages of manuscript are missing. Only a concluding portion of a dialogue between her heart's desire and her soul remains.[1] When Mary finishes relaying the teachings she has received from the Risen One, she falls silent. Then her conversation with the disciples resumes.

Andrew says, "Brothers, what is your opinion of what has been said? I for one do not believe that the Savior said these things, because these opinions seem so different from his thought" (Gospel of Mary 10:1–2, SV).

Mary has spoken from her experience, and Andrew has spoken from his, but the two impressions do not match; so what is really going on here?

As I read this remark by Andrew I am reminded of the old adage, "I know you believe you understand what you think I said; but I am not sure you realize that what you heard is not what I meant."

Another factor might also be at work, one that is next revealed by Peter, who asks, "Has the Savior spoken secretly to a woman and not openly so that we would all hear? Surely he did not wish to indicate that she is more worthy than we are?" (Gospel of Mary 10:3–4, SV).

If we consider the patriarchal attitudes of the time, we can recognize where Peter's objections originate.

Mary weeps and says, "Peter, my brother, what are you imagining about this? Do you think that I've made all this up secretly by myself or that I am telling lies about the Savior?" (Gospel of Mary 10:5, SV).

Now Levi, the first-century IRS man who has been transformed, moves the conversation more deeply into the feeling level and says, "Peter, you have a constant inclination to anger, and you are always ready to give way to it. And even now you are doing exactly that by questioning the woman as if you're her adversary. If the Savior considered her to be worthy, who are you to disregard her? For he knew her completely and loved her devotedly" (Gospel of Mary 10:7, SV).

In light of Mary Magdalene's close relationship with Jesus, is it any surprise that she not only is the first person to experience the Resurrected Jesus, but also is the one who understands the teachings most fully?

Levi, who seems most sensitive to understanding Mary and what she is revealing, shifts the message into mission by saying, "Instead (of responding angrily), we should be ashamed and, once we clothe ourselves with perfect humanity, we should do what we were commanded. We should announce the good news as the Savior ordered, and not be laying down any rules or making laws" (Gospel of Mary 10:11–13, SV).

As the seed of the true humanity sprouts and grows within the disciples, they begin to have something to share with others. Levi, in particular, begins putting his words into action, and *The Gospel of Mary* concludes in this way: "After he said these things, Levi left and began to announce the good news" (Gospel of Mary 10:14, SV).

10

Joanna's
Peak Experience

Joanna is a close friend of both Jesus and Mary Magdalene. The first time we meet her Luke describes her, in this scene:

> [Jesus] went on through cities and villages, proclaiming and bringing the good news of the kingdom of God. The twelve were with him, as well as some women who had been cured of evil spirits and infirmities: Mary, called Magdalene, from whom seven demons had gone out, and Joanna, the wife of Herod's steward Chuza, and Susanna, and many others, who provided for them out of their resources
> (Luke 8:1–3, NRSV).

This may be a short passage, but it provides a number of clues and questions. Joanna is married and has chosen to take time out to travel with Jesus. What might that have been like for her as a woman of the first century? How often does a woman leave her husband and home to go traveling with an itinerant teacher and his friends?

And what did the neighbors say when they heard that Joanna had left Chuza to go on the road with Jesus and his people? After all, she and Chuza are members of Herod's court and would normally have some status and some appearances to maintain.

More important, why did she decide to leave? From the story, we learn that she has experienced some healing by being with Jesus. Being "cured of evil spirits and infirmities" (Luke 8:2, NRSV) could mean any number of things. By today's standards, the first-century vocabulary for diagnosing and describing physical, emotional, and spiritual problems was very limited. Usually any problems out of the ordinary were identified as the work of an evil spirit or two. There are a range of possibilities, and no matter what our twenty-first century diagnosis might be, this one fact remains: she experiences healing. That in itself might be sufficient motivation to want to stay with Jesus and see what else she might experience and learn from him and his friends.

Whenever Joanna's name is mentioned, it comes immediately after Mary Magdalene's. Was she already a good friend of Mary Magdalene before they met Jesus? If so, which one might have introduced the other to him? Might they have influenced each other in their decisions to go traveling with the Teacher? Might some of their spontaneous decisions have been made in response to Jesus' charismatic personality?

When Joanna left home, what might she have left behind and what did she take with her? Luke tells us that the women used their resources to support Jesus and the Twelve. Although a contemporary woman leaving home could take her checkbook and credit cards, what resources would a first-century woman take with her?

Carla Ricci provides some insight into the economic and social status of first-century women:

> Since the condition of women in Palestine was generally one of deprivation, including in the economic sphere, how can one explain the finances that some of the women who followed Jesus were able to provide? Jewish law forbade a daughter to inherit from her father, and a wife from her husband. Not even the dowry assigned when a daughter became engaged was hers: up to the time the marriage vow was made, her father managed it and reaped the profits. Only if her husband divorced her or died did the woman come to own these goods. That women generally were not allowed to and did not own goods is indirectly confirmed by the fact that even objects found by chance belonged to their husband or father, that is, to the person to whom they themselves ultimately belonged.[1]

In order to help support the group, did Joanna sell some things to raise funds? Or did she leave home on good terms with Chuza, who kept funding her and her project? Or might she have gone home every so often, replenishing her finances each time? Or might Chuza have divorced her, freed her to go, and allowed her to take her dowry funds with her?

The sparse information in Luke stirs our imaginations and also raises questions in our own lives when we are considering making a break from our accustomed habits and friends to let our life take a new, possibly unknown, direction.

For Joanna, we really do not know exactly what happened. But a few things are clear: she had sufficient trust in her friend Mary Magdalene and Jesus to take the risk and go on a trip of unknown duration. It might be a new wonderful adventure, a complete disaster, or some of each. She also trusted her own intuition.

The next time Joanna is named in Luke's Gospel is at the tomb on the first Easter morning.

On the first day of the week, at early dawn, they came to the tomb, taking the spices that they had prepared. They found the stone rolled away from the tomb, but when they went in, they did not find the body. While they were perplexed about this, suddenly two men in dazzling clothes stood beside them. The women were terrified and bowed their faces to the ground, but the men said to them, "Why do you look for the living among the dead? He is not here, but has risen. Remember how he told you while he was still in Galilee, that the Son of Man must be handed over to sinners, and be crucified, and on the third day rise again." Then they remembered his words, and returning from the tomb, they told all this to the eleven and to all the rest. Now it was Mary Magdalene, Joanna, Mary the mother of James, and the other women with them who told this to the apostles.

(Luke 24:1–10, NRSV).

Was this the same group of women who signed on with Jesus at the beginning of his ministry? Might some women have joined along the way and might some have dropped out? For example, Susanna was mentioned at the beginning, but not here. Did she leave, or did the writer forget to include her? Most of the Gospels were written by males who neglected to name the women in the story as carefully as they did the names of other men. They also have an irritating habit of lumping all the females together as "the women." Suppose the story had been told primarily by women who simply mentioned the males as "the men"?

Because Joanna is named here in this empty-tomb scene, it would seem reasonable to assume that she stayed steady on the journey through Galilee on into the final days and the crucifixion when others scattered. Now she experiences the emptiness of the tomb. What will be next?

Apparently her friendship with Mary Magdalene remains constant, so it is also reasonable to assume that she is with her friend in some of the other scenes. She has come this far through all the excruciating pain; now it is time for some wondrous joy.

The Mountain of Divination and Joy

One of the many documents in the Nag Hammadi Library that contain stories of encounters with the Resurrected Jesus is *The Sophia of Jesus Christ.*

In this story, the Resurrected Jesus appears on a mountain. In mythic stories, whenever the setting is a mountain, you know immediately that something of major significance will occur. Here are some examples: Noah and the ark landing safely on Mount Ararat, Moses receiving the Commandments on Mount Sinai, Jesus delivering the Sermon on the Mount, the disciples with Jesus on the mountain of transfiguration, Jesus praying on the Mount of Olives.

The mountain in this story is named "Divination and Joy," which makes it doubly clear that something of great importance is about to occur. In this scene, Mary Magdalene is with six other women and twelve men disciples. As we have seen, Joanna is a friend of Mary Magdalene, who has accompanied her from the beginning and through the crucifixion of Jesus. It is more than likely that she is also present on the Mountain of Divination and Joy.

> When they gathered together, they were perplexed about the origin (or nature) of the universe, the plan, the holy providence, the power, the authorities, and concerning everything that the Savior does with them in the secret of the holy plan. The Savior appeared, not in his first form, but in the invisible spirit. And his form was like a great angel of light. And his likeness I must not describe. No mortal flesh can endure it, but only pure and perfect flesh like that which he taught us about on the mountain called "Of the Olives" in Galilee. And he said, "Peace to you! My peace I give to you!"
>
> (Sophia of Jesus Christ 91:1–20, NHL).

This is the typical greeting Jesus encouraged his disciples to use whenever entering a home (Luke 10:5) and the same one used in the story of the stilling of the waves (Mark 4:39). The Resurrected Jesus says "Shalom," which translates as "peace" and means much more than a good feeling. Shalom is peace with justice. It is the peace that goes beyond human understanding.

Hearing this greeting, Joanna, Mary Magdalene, and all the others "marveled and were afraid." Have you ever noticed how something can be wonderful and fearful at the same time? Both emotions often coexist; it seems one cannot have the marvel without the fear as well.

Seeing their response, the Savior laughs as Jesus did when he came up out of the waters of baptism (Gospel of Philip 74:29–31), and then asks three questions.

"What are you thinking about?" When Mary Magdalene hears this question, I wonder if she might recall her earlier vision when she heard the Resurrected Jesus saying, "Where the mind is, there is the treasure" (Gospel of Mary 7:3, SV). The Resurrected Jesus apparently knows he has touched inner thoughts, so he follows his first probing question with another, "Why are you perplexed?" Before anyone responds, the Resurrected Jesus takes his questioning to an even deeper level by asking, "What are you searching for?"

In this story, Philip is the first to respond, and the dialogue continues. After he and Matthew and Thomas make their responses and ask their questions, then Mary Magdalene takes her window of opportunity and begins posing her questions to the Risen One. In this resurrection appearance, the Resurrected Jesus questions the disciples, and they ask their questions as well.

At one point Mary Magdalene asks her three questions in rapid succession: "Holy Lord, where did your disciples come from? Where are they going? And what should they do here?"

One of the fascinating aspects of this conversation is that the Resurrected Jesus speaks of God the Father's consort, who is Sophia (Wisdom). During his baptism, Jesus came into a new relationship with God and could cry out, "Abba, Father!" Now the Resurrected Jesus reveals God as Mother as well as Father. All things come into being by the will of the Mother of the Universe.

In the Genesis creation stories, God creates by speaking. The Mother of the Universe creates through silence, the opposite of vocal expression. Could it be that Creation occurs through rhythmic patterns of spoken words and containers of silence? Might it be that God the Father and God the Mother are consorts working in concert?

11

You Went Away and Left Us!

Most people have heard of the Letter of James, but how many know *The Secret Book of James?* This book is part of the Nag Hammadi Library, which was hidden in the earth from the beginning of the fourth century until Muhammad Ali and his brother found it in 1945. In some translations you will find this book with the title *The Apocryphon of James.* An apocryphon is a writing containing secret meanings, so the most direct title in English is the one chosen by the Jesus Seminar scholars—*The Secret Book of James.*

More important, this book is secret because it contains teachings that are described as personal conversations between the Resurrected Jesus and the Twelve.

Dating *The Secret Book of James* is difficult, but an educated guess places it in the first half of the second century. James, the brother of Jesus, died in 62 C.E., so he did not write it. However, the book contains some teachings that are very early and may, indeed, spring from the experience of James with his Risen Brother.

The Secret Book of James relates that 550 days after his resurrection and immediately before his ascension, Jesus gave personal instruction to James and Peter. At the beginning of this book, the author says that "the twelve disciples used to sit together at the same time, remembering what the Savior had said to each one of them, whether secretly or openly, and setting it down in books."

James then says, "I was writing in my book—suddenly the Savior appeared, after he had departed from us, and while we were watching for him." You might expect that 550 days after the crucifixion James and Peter would be amazed and delighted to see him, but instead they say, "You went away and left us!"

This is a curious response, so what is really going on here? Surely they have been feeling the pain of his absence. When Jesus was with them, they could rely on him and his wisdom. Whenever they found themselves in a tough spot or needed help, or didn't know what to decide, they could ask Jesus. Now might they be angry at having to make decisions and shoulder responsibilities without him and his guidance?

[handwritten note in left margin: Who did write it?]

[handwritten note at bottom: They felt abandoned, unsure of themselves without Jesus]

48

After James and Peter say, "You went away and left us!" Jesus replies, "No, but I shall go to the place from which I have come. If you wish to come with me, come on!"

Then all the disciples answered, "If you bid us, we'll come!"

Jesus then replies, "Truly, I say to you, no one will enter the kingdom of heaven if I bid him, but rather because you yourselves are full. Let me have James and Peter, so that I may fill them."

The Savior then asks James and Peter a few questions: "Don't you want to be filled?" "Is your heart drunk?" "So don't you desire to be sober?"

The issue is not primarily about drinking to excess; rather, it is a spiritual question of what is in our hearts. What might it mean to have a drunken heart?

The conversation continues, and often the message of the Resurrected Jesus echoes and expands the teachings of the historical Jesus. Here are a few examples:

Jesus tells the story of the wise man building his house upon a rock and the foolish man building his house upon the sand. (Matt. 7:24–27). That story echoes and resounds in its retelling in The Secret Book of James: "I am made known to you building a house of great value to you, since you take shelter in it; likewise, it can support your neighbors' house when theirs is in danger of collapsing" (Secret Book of James 8:7, SV).

In both versions, you are the house. How are you built, and what is your foundation resting on? And what is going on inside your house?

The greater our own stability, the more we can make ourselves available to others when they are collapsing. The saying in *The Secret Book of James* expands the original teaching to include the neighbor's house and the building of community through mutual support.

The Risen One refers to stories previously told by Jesus and summarizes a few by saying, "It was enough for some people to pay attention to the teaching and understand 'the shepherds,' and 'the seed,' and 'the building,' and 'the lamps and the virgins,' and 'the wages of the workers,' and 'the silver coins,' and 'the woman'" (Secret Book of James 6:15, SV).

Then the Risen Christ adds:

"Become eager for instruction. For the first prerequisite for instruction is faith, the second is love, the third is works; now from these comes life. For instruction is like a grain of wheat. When they sowed it they had faith in it; and when it sprouted they loved it, because they envisioned many grains in place of one; and when they worked they were sustained, because they prepared it for food, then kept the rest in reserve to be sown. So it is possible for you to receive for yourselves the *kingdom of heaven*: unless you receive it through knowledge you will not be able to discover it."

(Secret Book of James 6:16–18, SV; *the kingdom of heaven* is NHL trans.)

The same kinds of metaphors that Jesus used are continued by the Risen Christ. One of my favorites is this.

> "Don't let heaven's domain wither away. For it is like a date palm shoot whose fruit fell down around it. It put forth buds, and when they blossomed, its productivity was caused to dry up. So it also is with the fruit that came from this singular root: when it was picked, fruit was gathered by many. Truly, this was good. Isn't it possible to produce new growth now? Can't you discover how?"
>
> (Secret Book of James 6:10–12, SV).

Those of us who are seeking personal growth can be encouraged by the teachings of the historic Jesus that are continued by the Resurrected Jesus, who reminds us of the tremendous potential already planted within us. We have the opportunity to become aware of the seed within us, to nourish it, and to bring its potential to fruition. *obligation?*

Now here is a teaching that may startle you at first: "Become better than I; be like the son of the Holy Spirit!" (Secret Book of James 5:6, SV). This teaching reminds me of a saying in the Gospel of John: "The one who believes in me will also do the works that I do and, in fact, will do greater works than these, because I am going to the Father" (John 14:12, NRSV).

Become better than Christ? Do more than Jesus? We have the living example and a sample of the work that is possible; now we carry the responsibility.

Repeatedly, Jesus calls our attention to the fact that the Kingdom of Heaven is here and living within us. Now the Resurrected Jesus warns us: "Do not make the kingdom of heaven a desert within you" (Secret Book of James 13:17, NHL).

The Secret Book of James contains a number of great one-liners suitable for printing out and posting on your refrigerator, near your computer, or some other convenient place. Here is a sample: "Pay attention to instruction, understand knowledge, love life" (Secret Book of James 6:27, SV).

The Beatitudes are in the Gospels of Matthew and Luke. *The Secret Book of James* adds a few more.

> "Blessed are you when you speak out fearlessly and obtain grace for yourself"
>
> (Secret Book of James 7:3, SV and NHL).

"Blessed are you who are on the Way to the Father!"
>	(Secret Book of James 8:9, SV and NHL conflated).

"Blessed are those who have known me"
>	(Secret Book of James 8:5, SV and NHL conflated).

"Blessed are you who have not seen, but have had faith"
>	(Secret Book of James 8:6, SV and NHL conflated).

Here is one more that may seem puzzling: "Blessed are you who have envisioned yourselves as the fourth one in heaven" (Secret Book of James 7:9, SV). There is no general agreement among the scholars as to what it means to be "the fourth one in heaven." Some of the sayings in *The Secret Book of James* are like koans; you have to meditate on them for a while in order to understand them. Whenever a saying from Jesus is puzzling, take time to savor it as you might a small glass of sherry or amaretto, and allow its meaning to gently slip into your soul and become part of the way you see life.[1]

12

Paul,
One Who Never Met Jesus

Apparently the man Saul, who is also known as Paul, never met Jesus of Nazareth before his crucifixion. Or if Paul did meet Jesus, we have no evidence of that fact. Saul's first contact comes after the crucifixion, when the followers of Jesus are claiming he has risen from the dead. Their claims are causing civil unrest everywhere they go. Saul sees this emerging movement as divisive within his Jewish religion. Any disturbances are likely to incur further repressive action from the occupying Roman forces.

Saul feels it is his duty to put an end to this problem. His attitude is "Nip it in the bud!" Filled with religious zeal and quite certain that he is doing the right thing, Saul gains authorization from the high priest and begins arresting the leaders of this disruptive movement. His work is efficient and successful.

Saul Becomes Paul

Then one day everything changes for Saul; he meets the Resurrected Jesus. As a result of this encounter, Saul makes a 180-degree turn in his thinking and in his behavior. In an act symbolic of his transformation, Saul changes his name to Paul. In a letter to friends in Galatia, Paul describes what happened to him:

> For I want you to know, brothers and sisters, that the gospel that was proclaimed by me is not of human origin; for I did not receive it from a human source, nor was I taught it, but I received it through a revelation of Jesus Christ.
>
> You have heard, no doubt, of my earlier life in Judaism. I was violently persecuting the church of God and was trying to destroy it. I advanced in Judaism beyond many among my people of the same age, for I was far more zealous for the traditions of my ancestors. But when God, who had set me apart before I was born and called me through

his grace, was pleased to reveal his Son to me, so that I might proclaim
him among the Gentiles . . .

(Gal. 1:11–16a, NRSV).

Paul puts his experience very succinctly; God reveals his Son to him. Paul
does not go into any further detail here. Another probably more familiar but
secondhand account of what happened to Saul is found in Luke's sequel to his
Gospel, The Acts of the Apostles:

Saul, still breathing threats and murder against the disciples of the
Lord, went to the high priest and asked him for letters to the synagogues at Damascus, so that if he found any who belonged to the
Way, men or women, he might bring them bound to Jerusalem. Now
as he was going along and approaching Damascus, suddenly a light
from heaven flashed around him. He fell to the ground and heard a
voice saying to him, "Saul, Saul, why do you persecute me?" He
asked, "Who are you, Lord?" The reply came, "I am Jesus, whom you
are persecuting. But get up and enter the city, and you will be told
what you are to do." The men who were traveling with him stood
speechless because they heard the voice but saw no one. Saul got up
from the ground, and though his eyes were open, he could see nothing; so they led him by the hand and brought him into Damascus.
For three days he was without sight, and neither ate nor drank.

(Acts 9:1–9, NHL).

I find it curious that the fuller account with more detail was written not
by Paul but by someone else. Did the writer of Acts interview Paul and obtain
more details than Paul had included in his own description? Or did the writer
elaborate on the story? As to what happened historically, we may never know
the answer to these questions. However, when we take the stories symbolically,
we can discover elements of a conversion process that have great value in regard
to significant turning points in our own lives.

In both accounts we see someone who fights with all his might against something he finds intolerable. His resistance becomes more and more intense until
one day it all comes to a head. Through direct confrontation with the Risen
Christ, Paul's energy, which has been directed in a negative way against Christ and
the gospel, is turned around and converted into positive energy for the gospel.
The results are clear—the rapid expansion of the church and a legacy of letters.

Have you noticed how love and hate are often the flip side of each other?
Sometimes in love relationships people fall madly in love but before long seem

to hate each other. If they have the tenacity and the courage, they can work through the intense Love-Hate feelings to a new and fresh relationship with ongoing commitment.

At times, a child who is very upset will say, "I hate you, mommy!" Hearing that can be devastating for a parent, but it can be dealt with. Often the parent has said "No" to what the child wanted. There is a clash of wills, and the child lashes out with the most hurtful thing that a child can say. With love, patience, and genuine dialogue, a parent and a child can work through the situation and become closer in the process.

You can work with love; you can work with hate. It is apathy that is the killer. Those who are apathetic in their relationships and those who are apathetic toward God have no feeling. They really don't care. I have seen people who appear so apathetic that if you were to hook up their soul to a monitor the way hearts are hooked up to a monitor in the hospital, the reading would be flat. Apathy may be the result of confusion, fear, or change, or an insufficient measure of faith.

Paul may be accused of many things, but apathy is not one of them. From all accounts, Paul does an about-face that can be a tremendous strain on the psyche. At the heart of the change is his encounter with the Resurrected Jesus. In the Acts account we are told that the immediate result is temporary blindness. This may have been literal blindness, or it may describe a major change in the way in which he sees things: blind to what he saw before, now open to seeing all of life with greater clarity.

As we might say today, how does Paul "process" this change? The Acts account tells us that three days later Paul experiences healing of his blindness through prayer and the laying on of hands. Then "for several days he was with the disciples in Damascus, and immediately he began to proclaim Jesus in the synagogues, saying, 'He is the Son of God'" (Acts 9:19b–20, NRSV).

In Paul's own account, he does not jump into his new way of life and ministry quite so quickly. Paul writes, "I did not confer with any human being, nor did I go up to Jerusalem to those who were already apostles before me, but I went away at once into Arabia, and afterwards I returned to Damascus" (Gal. 1:16b–17, NRSV).

Paul says he took time out in Arabia, which reminds us of the experience of Jesus who, after his powerful baptism experience, took forty days in the wilderness to process his experience and deal with questions confronting him before doing anything else.

For anyone going through a major life change, there are many choices, including whether to jump into the new thing right away or to take some time out to sort through the changes and their implications.

According to Paul's own account, he did take time out in the desert of Arabia—for how long he does not say. Then he returns to Damascus and remains there for a while. After that, Paul says:

Then after three years I did go up to Jerusalem to visit Cephas and stayed with him fifteen days; but I did not see any other apostle except James the Lord's brother. In what I am writing to you, before God, I do not lie! Then I went into the regions of Syria and Cilicia, and I was still unknown by sight to the churches of Judea that are in Christ; they only heard it said, "The one who formerly was persecuting us is now proclaiming the faith he once tried to destroy." And they glorified God because of me.

Then after fourteen years I went up again to Jerusalem with Barnabas, taking Titus along with me. I went up in response to a revelation.

(Gal. 1:18–2:2a, NRSV)

Comparing the Teachings of Jesus and the Teachings of Paul

Paul's ministry is detailed in his letters that have come down to us and in the Book of Acts. The life and ministry of Paul has been given innumerable reviews in countless commentaries, and I will make no attempt to summarize.

However, one or two questions catch my imagination. Because Paul apparently did not know Jesus or hear his teachings, what continuities and discontinuities might there be between the life and teachings of Jesus and the life and teachings of Paul after his experience with the Resurrected Jesus?

I keep in mind some of the central teachings of Jesus, begin scanning the writings of Paul, and what do I find?

At the heart of Jesus' teaching is the phrase that, rendered in English, is usually translated as "the Kingdom of the Father," "the Kingdom of Heaven," "the Kingdom of God," or as some scholars are suggesting, "the Community of God."

The Acts of the Apostles describes Paul's preaching in Corinth. "He entered the synagogue and for three months spoke out boldly, and argued persuasively about the kingdom of God" (Acts 19:8, NRSV).

On another occasion, Acts quotes Paul as saying, "And now I know that none of you, among whom I have gone about proclaiming the kingdom, will ever see my face again" (Acts 20:25, NRSV). And again in the last chapter of Acts, "From morning until evening [Paul] explained the matter to them, testifying to the kingdom of God and trying to convince them about Jesus both from the law of Moses and from the prophets" (Acts 28:23b, NRSV).

In his own letters are places where Paul says what he thinks the Kingdom of God is not about: "For the kingdom of God is not food and drink but righteousness and peace and joy in the Holy Spirit" (Rom. 14:17, NRSV); "For the kingdom of God depends not on talk but on power" (I Cor. 4:20, NRSV).

Paul gives a list of people he thinks will "not inherit the kingdom of God. Do not be deceived! Fornicators, idolaters, adulterers, male prostitutes, sodomites, thieves, the greedy, drunkards, revilers, robbers—none of these will inherit the kingdom of God" (I Cor. 6:10, NRSV). A similar list appears in Paul's letter to the Galatians (Gal. 5:19–21).

Jesus, on the other hand, does not have such a list. Instead, there is the famous story of his being with the woman taken in adultery and about to be stoned. Jesus says, "Let anyone among you who is without sin be the first to throw a stone at her" (John 8:7, NRSV). The people surrounding the woman and Jesus got the message, dropped their stones, and went away. I wonder if Paul ever heard this story. If he had, would he be so quick to throw these exclusionary accusations at people on his categorical list?

In his letter to the Romans, Paul instructs people to be "subject to the governing authorities. . . . Pay to all what is due them—taxes to whom taxes are due, revenue to whom revenue is due, respect to whom respect is due, honor to whom honor is due." (Rom. 13:3,7, NRSV) Paul is a Roman citizen, so it is not surprising that he sides with the Roman administration that is occupying Israel at this time.

Paul has a picture of Christ in which he says, "Then comes the end, when [Christ] hands over the kingdom to God the Father, after he has destroyed every ruler and every authority and power. For he must reign until he has put all his enemies under his feet" (I Cor. 15:24–25, NRSV).

Recall Jesus' many teachings that speak about loving your enemies, praying for those who persecute you, returning good for evil, turning the other cheek. Maybe Paul never heard those parts of the message. Or if someone did report these sayings of Jesus, was Paul ignoring them?

Paul uses the phrase "Kingdom of God," but does he mean the same thing that Jesus means? So often Paul seems to speak of an external kingdom that is hard to distinguish from that of the Roman Empire, which enforces its power.

Much of the history of the Christian religion seems based on an interpretation of Paul's concepts of domination in the name of God. It worked for Constantine and the Roman Empire. It worked for Charlemagne and the Holy Roman Empire. It worked for the British Empire. It seems to be working quite well for the Great American Empire, which is well on its way to global domination, often in the name of "God." Domination, exploitation, sanctions to the point of genocide, and high-tech warfare are often justified as being necessary when done in the name of God's rule!

In some respects, there are enormous discontinuities between Jesus' teachings and Paul's teachings. The Son of Man (Seed of True Humanity) concept that is central for Jesus is nowhere to be found in Paul. "Son of God" is often used, but the emphasis on Son of Man, the Authentic Human Being, is missing. Paul often refers to the "Lord Jesus Christ." He uses the name of Jesus, but where is he working from the teachings of Jesus?

Yet Paul has a powerful experience of the Resurrected Jesus, not just in his conversion, the turning point already discussed, but further in his consistent focus on the process of death and resurrection. In I Corinthians 15 and in many other places Paul affirms the necessity of dying to sin and rising to a new life in Christ. This is a process that needs to occur regularly; as Paul says, "I die every day."

To be fair to Paul, there are some similarities between his teachings and those of Jesus. His famous chapter 13 of First Corinthians about love, often chosen by couples to be read at their weddings, is a masterpiece that matches rather well with the teachings of Jesus: being patient, kind, forgiving, and not keeping score of wrongs. Paul acknowledges his own personal struggle quite openly:

> I do not understand my own actions. For I do not do what I want, but I do the very thing I hate. . . . I can will what is right, but I cannot do it. For I do not do the good I want, but the evil I do not want is what I do. . . . When I want to do what is good, evil lies close at hand. For I delight in the law of God in my inmost self, but I see in my members another law at war with the law of my mind, making me captive to the law of sin that dwells in my members. Wretched man that I am! Who will rescue me from this body of death?
>
> (Rom. 7:15–24, NRSV).

> We know that the whole creation has been groaning in labor pains until now; and not only the creation, but we ourselves, who have the first fruits of the Spirit, groan inwardly while we wait for adoption, the redemption of our bodies. . . . Likewise the Spirit helps us in our weakness; for we do not know how to pray as we ought, but that very Spirit intercedes with sighs too deep for words.
>
> (Rom. 8:22–26, NRSV).

Those of us who have been through our own personal struggles and inner conflicts can relate to what Paul is saying here. We might even feel some compassion for him and some appreciation for his speaking openly about his struggles rather than keeping them to himself.

So what shall we do with Paul and his writings? Personally, I admire him for his passion, his sincerity, and his struggle in finding the words to express what he believes the gospel is all about. However, I do not feel obliged to agree with all his conclusions. Let the life and teachings of Jesus show us the way of life. When Paul's teachings are in harmony with those of Jesus, embrace them and use them. When they are in contradiction, set them aside. Reading Paul requires wisdom. The symbol for Wisdom (Sophia) is salt. Paul is useful so long as we remember to take him with a grain of salt.

Whenever Paul's teaching diverges from those of Jesus, it may help to remember that Paul did not have the benefit of knowing Jesus in person, nor did he have the Gospels to read, and that makes a very big difference.

Prayer of Paul the Apostle

I close this chapter with The Prayer of the Apostle Paul, which is on the front flyleaf of the first book in the Nag Hammadi Library. The prayer was not written by Paul but has the same kind of spiritual intensity. It was composed in his honor by an anonymous author sometime toward the end of the second century or the beginning of the third.

References to "First-born" and "First-begotten" are to Christ. Pleroma means "fullness." Paraclete means "advocate" or "intercessor."

This prayer gives expression to a deep desire to know All that IS! This prayer is one I feel deeply; I include it for you with great joy:

My Redeemer, redeem me, for I am yours: from you have I come forth.
You are my mind: bring me forth!
You are my treasure-house: open for me!
You are my fullness: take me to you!
You are my repose: give me the perfection that cannot be grasped!

I invoke you, the one who is and preexisted, by the name which is exalted above every name, through Jesus Christ the Lord of Lords, the king of the ages: give me your gifts which you do not regret through the Son of man, the Spirit, the Paraclete of truth.

Give me authority when I ask you; give healing for my body when I ask you through the Evangelist, and redeem my eternal light-soul and my spirit.

And the First-born of the Pleroma of grace—reveal him to my mind!

Grant what no angel-eye has seen and no archon-ear has heard and what has not entered into the human heart, which came to be angelic and came to be after the image of the psychic God when it was formed in the beginning, since I have faith and hope. And place upon me your beloved, elect, and blessed greatness, the First-born, the First-begotten, and the wonderful mystery of your house; for yours is the power and the glory and the blessing and the greatness for ever and ever. Amen.

13

Resurrected Jesus
as Pearl Merchant

The scene for the next experience of the Resurrected Jesus is a small city in the midst of the sea—in other words, an island reachable only by boat. Peter and the other apostles sail there, go ashore, and look for lodging. This resurrection story is found in *The Acts of Peter and the Twelve Apostles*, a second-century document in the Nag Hammadi Library.

The Merchant Cries, "Pearls! Pearls!"

Peter is the narrator, and he tells us the following:

> A man came out wearing a cloth bound around his waist, and a gold belt girded it. Also a napkin was tied over his chest, extending over his shoulders and covering his head and his arms.
>
> I was staring at the man, because he was beautiful in his form and stature. There were four parts of his body which I saw: the tops of his feet, and a part of his chest, and the palm of his hands, and his visage. These things I was able to see. A book cover like those of my books was in his left hand. A staff of styrax wood was in his right hand. His voice was resounding as he slowly spoke, crying out in the city, "Pearls! Pearls!"
> (Acts of Peter and the Twelve Apostles 2:10–32, NHL).

So his body is completely covered except for his hands, his feet, his side, and his face. Exposed are the four places where Jesus had been nailed to the cross and the fifth where his body had been pierced by a spear. But this is not the tortured and bloodied body, but one that is beautiful in form and stature.

Thinking that here is a man of the city who can give him directions, Peter says, "My brother and my friend!" He answers and says, "Rightly did you say, 'My brother and my friend.' What is it you seek from me?" Peter replies, "I ask you about lodging for me and the brothers also, because we are strangers here." He says to Peter, "For this reason have I myself just said, 'My brother and my friend,' because I also am a fellow stranger like you" (Acts of Peter and the Twelve Apostles 2:35–3:11, NHL).

They are addressing each other as brother and as friend; apparently at some level they recognize each other, yet not in the same way that Peter and Jesus had known each other. They are both strangers in town and are in some degree strangers to each other. But additional clues to the identity of this handsome man are being given, this time by his repeating his cry, "Pearls! Pearls!"

The rich men of the city hear his voice and come out of their hidden storerooms. Some look out from the storerooms of their houses. Others look out from their upper windows.

They notice that he has no backpack, no bundle, and they assume that they could not gain anything from him. They are irritated by him, and try not to pay any more attention to him. They return to their storerooms, saying, "This man is mocking us" (Acts of Peter and the Twelve Apostles 3:31, NHL).

Then the poor of the city hear his voice and come to the man who sells pearls. They say:

> "Please take the trouble to show us the pearl so that we may, then, see it with our own eyes. For we are the poor. And we do not have this price to pay for it. But allow us to say to our friends that we saw a pearl with our own eyes." He answered saying to them, "If it is possible, you yourselves come to my city, so that I may not only show it before your very eyes, but give it to you for nothing."
> (Acts of Peter and the Twelve Apostles 4:5–15, NHL, Third Edition)

Pearls of Wisdom from Jesus

I wonder if Peter and the others might have recalled the teaching of Jesus about pearls. Jesus said: "The kingdom of heaven is like a merchant in search of fine pearls; on finding one pearl of great value, he went and sold all that he had and bought it" (Matt. 13:45, NRSV).

What good would it do the merchant who invests all his capital into one pearl, especially if he is going to keep it? But suppose this pearl is more valuable than anything else in life. That may be what Jesus is trying to get across about the inestimable value of the Kingdom of Heaven.

Just as Jesus had given his teachings about the Kingdom of Heaven that is more precious, more desirable than the finest of pearls, now this man is offering pearls to all who have the humility to accept them. Who is this man?

As the story progresses we learn his name. He is called Lithargoel, which means "a lightweight stone that gleams like the eye of a gazelle." In other words, a pearl! Just as Jesus taught about pearls, so now the Resurrected Jesus appears as a Pearl Merchant who is himself the pearl.

The Resurrected Jesus has become the One of great value who now continues to offer the pearls of wisdom he previously offered in his teachings. During the life of the historic Jesus there were limitations to his sphere of influence. He could be in only one place at a time. However, the Resurrected Jesus is present simultaneously in many places continuing to proclaim his teachings.

One might say that Jesus, his experience and teachings, is the original irritant around which the Pearl of Wisdom is created. The Resurrected Jesus continues to offer the Wisdom Pearls. The rich who are self-satisfied close their doors and hearts to these pearls and continue storing away whatever they think is valuable.

But the poor, those who recognize their need for wisdom and are open to receive, will be given the pearls of priceless value, simply for the heartfelt asking. Lithargoel is still among us in a wide variety of disguises, crying, "Pearls! Pearls!"

Jesus is quite clear about the asking when he says, "Ask, and it will be given you; search and you will find; knock, and the door will be opened for you" (Matt. 7:7, NRSV).

The teaching is expanded in the version found in *The Gospel of Thomas.* Jesus said, "Those who seek should not stop seeking until they find. When they find, they will be disturbed. When they are disturbed, they will marvel, and will rule over all, and when they rule, they will rest" (Gospel of Thomas 2, Greek, SV).

The Gospel of Thomas version reveals more of the process involved in seeking. Have you ever looked or searched for something or someone? When you found what you thought you were looking for, what happened?

For example, a new person in your life can be exciting but also troubling because your life, your time, and your priorities are all influenced and rearranged. Or a new concept may cause rethinking many other ideas. You may find yourself facing the question of whether or not to let go of long-held opinions, biases, and even prejudices.

When the time of troubling is over, you may feel rather surprised and amazed. Keep moving further with the process and you may reach the higher point of "ruling over the all": that is the new perspective.

The final step in the process is rest, blessed rest. This means more than relaxing and taking it easy. It means resting in life, being in rhythm with that which IS. Like a skilled skier gliding down the slopes almost effortlessly, or an experienced sailor knowing how to catch the wind and adjust the sails, so we rest in a new way of living.

Once the cycle is completed, it may be time to begin again with fresh seeking, finding, troubling, marveling, ruling over all, and resting again!

What really prompts us to seek in the first place? Often an irritant, small or large, gets us started. That irritant could very well be the beginning of wisdom, just as a bit of sand or other irritant in an oyster is what starts the process of forming a pearl.

Recall, once again, this saying from Jesus: "The kingdom of heaven is like a merchant in search of fine pearls; on finding one pearl of great value, he went and sold all that he had and bought it" (Matt. 13:45, NRSV).

If we are to find the Kingdom of Heaven, there is actually a cost—the willingness to sell all.

What might be involved in "selling all"? Shall we be like St. Francis of Assisi and literally give up everything we have? Might there be anything else besides possessions we are expected to give up for the Kingdom of Heaven?

Suppose we were to start with asking what is, in fact, most precious to us?

Beyond "things," what might be included? Suppose it is another person, a parent, lover, mate, or child; are we expected to give them up as well?

Suppose our most precious possession is our own life; are we to give that up? Jesus said, "Those who want to save their life will lose it, and those who lose their life for my sake, and for the sake of the gospel, will save it" (Mark 8:35, NRSV).

Does "selling all" mean that Jesus is teaching us literally to give up everything: possessions, relationships, even our lives? In fact, when we die all will be taken from us. As the Burial Office in *The Book of Common Prayer* (1928) reminds us, "We brought nothing into this world, and it is certain we can carry nothing out. The Lord giveth, and the Lord hath taken away; blessed be the name of the Lord!"

So we have a choice. Either we wait until everything, even our very existence, is taken from us. Or can we practice early the attitude of giving up everything? What do we actually own? Consider the things we possess. Even if we worked for them, did we create them? Everything that exists actually has only one owner, the Source of All, who loans them to us for a while until we return them. And do we own other people? When one person acts as though he or she owns another, trouble is inevitable! And ourselves, did we make ourselves? To be realistic, all we are and all that we have are gifts to us, for a while.

Once we give up the ridiculous notion of owning anything, then a curious thing happens. We are given back things, relationships, and ourselves, but in a new way. The Buddhist notion of "detachment" may be very close to what Jesus is teaching us.

So Jesus teaches us that when we "sell all" we are given the Kingdom of Heaven. Where is heaven? Is it some sort of "Life after Death"? One popular notion for a very long time has been that if we grin and bear it through this life, then we will go to another place called "heaven." If so, where is heaven located?

Is this what Jesus is really teaching us? Listen again and we find that Jesus says, "The Kingdom of the Father is inside you and outside you" (Gospel of Thomas 3, SV and NHL conflated). Over and over again he is saying that it is here right now, inside us and in our relationships. Or, as my wife, Grace, says, "within, around, and beyond us."

14

Resurrected Jesus
as Physician

The family, friends, and followers of Jesus do not usually recognize the Resurrected Jesus at first glance. We have already seen several of his disguises: a gardener to Mary Magdalene, a traveler to Cleopas, a powerful Holy Spirit to his mother Mary and the assembled community on Pentecost, a pearl merchant named Lithargoel to Peter.

Just as Jesus spoke of the Kingdom of God as a pearl, so the Resurrected Jesus not only offers the pearl but is the pearl, Lithargoel. As the story continues in *The Acts of Peter and the Twelve Apostles* (NHL), this same Lithargoel now comes as a physician.

Lithargoel's staff is made of styrax wood, which is wood of an aromatic gum tree. "The resin, which is produced by old trees, was an ingredient of the holy anointing oil. Medicinally, it was used to treat coughs and as an ointment for swelling. It also became an ingredient of perfume."[1] A staff of styrax wood identifies someone as a healer, just as a stethoscope around the neck quickly identifies someone as a medical person today. Lithargoel carries the staff not for assistance but as a symbol of healing and for spreading a sweet aroma.

Tucked under Lithargoel's arm is an unguent box. A young disciple carrying a pouch full of medicine follows along.

No one recognizes Lithargoel until he calls Peter by name. Peter is frightened; how does this stranger know his name? Lithargoel answers, "I want to ask you who gave the name Peter to you?" And Peter replies, "It was Jesus Christ, the son of the living God. He gave this name to me."

Lithargoel reveals who he is by saying, "It is I. Recognize me, Peter." He loosens his garment, revealing his identity by showing the wound in his side.

Two things change the nonrecognition into awareness. The Resurrected Jesus shows his side, as in an earlier story on the first Easter (John 20:19ff). He also calls Peter by name. Peter recognizes the voice just as in the garden Mary Magdalene hears her name called and then recognizes the Risen One.

The Resurrected Jesus continues to call us by name. The next time you wake up in the middle of the night with the feeling that someone is calling you, pay attention and answer with whatever words come to your lips, "Yes, Lord, what do you want from me?"

Peter is frightened when he is called by name; any encounter with the Resurrected Jesus now can also be frightening at first. All kinds of questions and feelings can run through a person's mind and heart.

Peter and the other disciples prostrate themselves on the ground and worship him. Then he stretches forth his hand and causes them to stand. With their heads bowed, they speak humbly and say, "What you wish we will do. But give us power to do what you wish at all times."

The Lord gives them the pouch of medicine and says, "Heal all the sick of the city who believe in my name." Peter is afraid to reply to him for the second time. He signals to John who is beside him, "You talk this time." John answers, "Lord, before you we are afraid to say many words. But it is you who asks us to practice this skill. We have not been taught to be physicians. How then will we know how to heal bodies as you have told us?"

Lithargoel replies, "Rightly have you spoken, John, for I know that the physicians of this world heal what belongs to the world. The physicians of souls, however, heal the heart. Heal the bodies first, therefore, so that through the real powers of healing for their bodies, without medicine of the world, they may believe in you, that you have power to heal the illnesses of the heart also." (Quotations in the paragraphs above are from The Acts of Peter and the Twelve Apostles 9:10—11:26, NHL.)

Essentially, the Resurrected Jesus is saying to his friends: now it is your turn to continue the ministry of healing that I had before. You are to heal not only the body, but the heart as well. Which comes first: the body or the heart? The interconnection between the two was known for many years as psychosomatic medicine. More recently, the most common term is holistic medicine.

Each human being is both an individual and a member of the larger body of humanity. Followers of Jesus are expected to become aware of their being members of the Body of Christ, commissioned with the ministry of enabling the wholeness of individuals, society, and the whole earth.

Jesus as the Primary Model for How to Enable Healing

The central purpose of the ministry of Jesus can be summed up in one sentence from his own lips: "I must proclaim the good news of the kingdom of God . . . for I was sent for this purpose" (Luke 4:43, NRSV).

Jesus has a message to proclaim that catches the attention of people both then and now because it has an authentic ring. His teaching originates in his direct experience with the Living God. He knows what he is talking about. People watch him and observe that he lives what he teaches.

Who we are and what we do always speak louder than our words. With Jesus there is a consistency between who he is, the way he lives, and what he has to say. The results of this inner and outer consistency in Jesus' life often bring about healing in the lives of people.

As a direct result of being with Jesus, the blind are able to see—not just those who had literal blindness, but also those whose doors of perception needed cleansing. Their third eye begins to see more clearly.

The deaf are able to hear—not just those whose literal hearing has declined, but also those who have been deaf to the voice of God. They discover that their third ear is now working.

The lame are able to walk freely—not just those who have difficulty getting around, but those whose hearts have become so battered that they have difficulty putting one foot in front of another.

Those who are in prison are set free—not just those serving time for the state, but those imprisoned by their own fears, guilts, anxieties, and delusions.

One of the strongest and most encouraging stories in the Gospels is that of the Gerasene demoniac who is chained and left out in the wilderness. No one will have anything to do with him, but Jesus brings him the healing he needs to restore his soul, regain his balance, and begin living freely (Luke 8:26–39).

The stories go on and on, and the Source of the healing is very clear. Jesus is not a magician with powers to zap. Instead, Jesus is the catalyst for restoring the power of the Spirit already dwelling within people. Jesus calls out the Son of Man within to be healed and restored to right mind. Jesus is very clear about how healing occurs as he says, "Your faith has made you well" (Matt. 9:22, RSV).

One of the most fascinating things for me about Jesus' ministry of teaching and healing is how short it is. From his baptism when his ministry begins to the day of his death is no more than two or three years.

In the Gospels we have many accounts of Jesus' healing ministry, and what we have is no doubt only a small sample of what was going on. Jesus lives a rhythm of prayer and ministry with people that is powerful and effective.

His death was supposed to put a stop to his ministry. The resurrection of Christ surprises everybody, including, I suspect, even Jesus himself. Apparently Jesus also sensed that the Spirit would enable others to do all that he had done and more: "I swear to God, anyone who believes in me will perform the works I perform and will be able to perform even greater feats, because I'm on my way to the Father" (John 14:12, SV).

The healing ministry of Jesus is rapidly expanding. The Spirit that had been in Jesus is now being released without the former limitations. The Resurrected Jesus is capable of filling countless others simultaneously and in a variety of ways.

How Are We Supposed to Do This Healing?

The Resurrected Jesus appears as a physician, hands the disciples a pouch of medicine, and says, "Heal all the sick of the city who believe in my name."

John replies, "We have not been taught to be physicians. How then will we know how to heal bodies as you have told us?"

I certainly understand John's feeling. For nearly four decades I served as a parish priest. I know how to celebrate liturgy with people. I am a student and a teacher. I can review holy writings and compile an anthology for daily use. I can administer a parish and do my best to keep it steady through stormy seas. I am a pastor and can walk with people through the changes, chances, and choices of this mortal life. I can do a lot of things, but I am not a physician. I went to seminary, not to medical school.

There are physicians, surgeons, specialists of every sort and description from acupuncture to X-ray. There are psychologists, psychiatrists, analysts, therapists, counselors, and spiritual directors. Those with special gifts and training, not the ordinary person, have the responsibilities for healing.

Unless you are one of the aforementioned people, you may feel as I do that John says it for us, "We have not been taught to be physicians. How then will we know how to heal bodies as you have told us?" The Resurrected Jesus has an answer for John and for us:

> "Rightly have you spoken, John, for I know that the physicians of this world heal what belongs to the world. The physicians of souls, however, heal the heart. Heal the bodies first, therefore, so that through the real powers of healing for their bodies, without medicine of the world, they may believe in you, that you have power to heal the illnesses of the heart also."
>
> (Acts of Peter and the Twelve Apostles 11:15–26, NHL)

Does that help? Think about it. We are not expected to be diagnosticians, prescribe medicine, set bones, perform surgery, or administer laser or radiation treatments. No, all we have to do is heal the illnesses of the heart! So I want to ask the Risen Christ another question and say, "You expect me to heal illnesses of the heart? That can be even more difficult and complex than setting bones."

And then I hear some reassurance, "I will heal illnesses of the heart through you." It is a comfort and strength to know that the Resurrected Jesus is the healer. Our task, then, is to pay attention to those occasions and relationships where we can be part of Christ's healing ministry!

The Resurrected Jesus expects ordinary people like us to make ourselves available as channels for the healing grace of Christ. This is quite amazing and humbling. To be humble is to be humus—close to the earth! No inflation of our egos as superhealers is necessary. Yet Resurrected Jesus can and will use us—first by bringing about an increase of the healing of our own heart illnesses and simultaneously as partners in ministries of healing.

Four Essential Ingredients for Healing Ministry

There are four essential ingredients for growth in the healing process. They are stated clearly in *The Gospel of Philip*:

> Farming in the world requires the cooperation of four essential elements. A harvest is gathered into the barn only as a result of the natural action of water, earth, wind, and light. God's farming likewise has four elements—faith, hope, love, and knowledge. Faith is our earth, that in which we take root. And hope is the water through which we are nourished. Love is the wind through which we grow. Knowledge then is the light through which we ripen. Grace exists in four ways: it is earthborn; it is heavenly; it comes from the highest heaven; and it resides in truth.
>
> (Gospel of Philip 79:18–33, NHL)

Faith: A better word may be trust. I am continually saddened whenever I see people who have difficulty trusting. Trust is very precious. It starts with experiences like a little child learning to walk by putting a hand into the hand of a parent. It continues through other trusting relationships when we care for one another and are supportive of one another in countless ways.

What happens when trust is broken, when faith seems not to be returned to us? Do we feel hurt and become bitter? Do we become disillusioned? Eventually we may discover that there is only one essential place to put our trust and that is in God, the Source of our life.

When our primary trust is clear, then we can become more trusting of others. We can become free of the expectation that trust must be reciprocated. We can discover how to be trusting of others whether they deserve it or not. We can also learn how to go through those times when our trust is abused. We have some choices: to approach others with suspicion and to trust no one until we feel they are reliable; or we can initiate trust and become willing to take the risk of its not being returned.

I have the feeling Jesus consistently puts trust into others. We are told that he prays all night and then selects disciples, including one who betrays him, another who denies him, and others who are sometimes strong and sometimes very weak, especially when the pressure is on and they just wander off. Our model for trusting is clearly in the life of Jesus.

In the healing stories, trust functions in a variety of ways. Sometimes it is the person being healed, as in the scene where Jesus says to a woman with him at dinner, "Your trust has saved you; go in peace" (Luke 7:50, SV). Sometimes it is the faith of a parent for a child, or friends bringing a paralyzed person to the place of healing. The accounts in the Gospels provide a rich selection of situations where faith operates effectively in bringing healing. Genuine faith includes taking responsibility for our health and seeking medical advice from reliable medical professionals. Their skill and medicines may contribute to our healing.

Hope: Now hope, like faith, is a gift. It is essential for the healing process. Sometimes religion teaches people that if they believe and hope enough, they will be surely healed of cancer, of heart disease, of a broken heart, of AIDS, of anything! Is that really true?

Trust in God—regardless. That trust may or may not bring the desired results. But there is a certain kind of paradox. Being able to say wholeheartedly, "I trust you, Lord, whether or not I am healed of this" can make a great difference. By letting go of our anxieties, we release all the healing potential of our system. We may recover or go into remission.

One thing is quite clear—the Resurrected Jesus says, "I am with you always, to the end of the age" (Matt. 28:20, NRSV). As one age ends, the Resurrected Jesus is right there again as the next age is being ushered in. Knowing Christ provides the bonus of hope.

Hope really is a bonus. Trying to talk ourselves into being hopeful usually doesn't work. But forget about being hopeful, keep gently trusting in the Way Jesus shows us, and you may have a surprise. You may find yourself being hopeful as well.

Love: We all know what love can do for healing—and how destructive the lack of love can be. There is a particularly bitter country song of two people breaking up. One says to the other, "Here's a quarter, call someone who cares."

Suppose we are in a position to be a friend for someone else who is going through a bitter time. Christ's supportive love through us can, in fact, make a difference. We may even be in a position to suggest to someone else that it is time to place their trust in the Resurrected Jesus, who shows us the Way.

Knowledge: The fourth ingredient for healing, knowledge, is to know Christ, to experience that presence within ourselves and one another; there is no adequate way to describe it, but there is nothing more real.

Our task is to communicate the faith, hope, love, and knowledge of Christ, to be available as part of the process for others as well as ourselves. Through prayer, conversations, phone calls, E-mails, letters, and cards at the right time, through actions both practical and symbolic, we are part of the healing process.

You may or may not know the results of your part in the process, but being available to Christ is all that really matters.

How many people there are who need healing of hearts, mending of heartache! How many are in need of community and of knowing where they belong—knowing that someone in this world cares about them. They also need a place where they can share in support and healing for others.

This is precisely where the community of Christ comes into play. There is great value to smaller communities of the Resurrected Jesus because within them are opportunities for people to reach out and connect with one another, to walk with each other, to share joys and sorrows.

This healing ministry of community takes care and skill. When do we simply provide space without invading someone else's life? When do we provide a listening ear? When do we do something practical?

And how do we know? We can keep praying the same prayer the disciples prayed, "What you wish we will do. But give us power to do what you wish at all times." The power of the Holy Spirit is readily available to us as needed in the moment. *And, be not agraied*

Signs and Wonders

In the longer ending of the Gospel of Mark is this rather curious passage: "These signs will accompany those who believe: in my name they will cast out demons; they will speak in new tongues; they will pick up serpents, and if they drink any deadly thing, it will not hurt them; they will lay their hands on the sick, and they will recover" (Mark 16:17–18, RSV).

Whenever someone seems to be out of control and possessed by other forces, first-century people might consider them possessed by demons. And what might we call those demons today? The same phenomenon occurs in our time and is given new names: addictions, compulsions, complexes, dysfunctions of every sort and description.

When working with a demon-possessed person, Jesus would often ask, "What is your name?" He would call the demon by name and ask what the demon had to say. The same process is at work today when a therapist is able to identify and call by name the disorder that has been overpowering.

Someone at a meeting of Alcoholics Anonymous will say, "My name is Bill; I am an alcoholic." By identifying the symptom, one can begin to work the twelve-step program toward healing. Someone else being able to say, "I have an obsessive-compulsive disorder" is a way of identifying the problem. The process of becoming free begins.

Speaking in new tongues is a common experience these days, not only in the charismatic movement but for many who pray in the Spirit, run out of words to say what they feel, and begin praying freely in a tongue not consciously learned. The Pandora's box of the psyche is opening up, tremendous release is felt, and much significant material is tumbling out in need of recognition and integration.

What about the serpents? Some take snake handling quite literally and actually work with poisonous snakes as part of their worship. When a member dies of snake bite, the remaining members say it was because the person did not have enough faith.[2] This is what can happen when symbols are taken too literally.

A symbolic approach would look for the recurring symbol of the serpent in Holy Scripture for its meaning. In the Garden of Eden, it is the serpent who has a very necessary function—to present the choices. In the wilderness, Moses holds up a bronze serpent for the people to see, and they know they have choices to make in their journey through the wilderness. In the teachings of Jesus we are reminded to be "wise as serpents and innocent as doves" (Matt. 10:16, NRSV). Whenever a serpent appears in a story, someone has to make a decision. Handling serpents means that when the power of the Resurrected Jesus is alive within us, we become better at handling our decisions.

And what might be involved in "drinking a deadly thing"? On the night before his crucifixion, Jesus in Gethsemane is feeling the pressures of what might soon happen. He is praying, "Take this cup from me! But it's not what I want that matters, but what you want" (Mark 14:36, SV). What do you think that cup might represent? And what might it have contained for Jesus? How was he able to take and drink it regardless of the consequences?

What might be in some of the cups offered to us? Might there be times in life to accept even the bitter cup? In the Spirit of the Resurrected Jesus may we find how to handle the cups that life serves us, no matter what they contain?

And then comes one more sign following the resurrection: the "laying on of hands." The practice of prayer and laying on of hands for healing has been revived in a wide variety of ways: toward the end of the nineteenth century in Japan with Dr. Usui and the Reiki movement, at the turn of the twentieth century with the beginning of the Pentecostal movement, in the 1960s with the spreading of the Charismatic Renewal, and more recently with the New Age movement. Healing through laying on of hands today involves a wide range of practices, with everything from intense prayer meetings to healing massage and watsu, a form of massage given in a pool of warm water. The power of touch to heal is being revived. How much is authentic and a source of genuine healing? How much is unrealistic and a source of false hopes? Our task is discovering how to distinguish genuine practices from those that may be naive or counterfeit.

15

Resurrected Jesus as Child, Young Person, Servant, Old Man

As we have seen, one of the repeating themes in the resurrection accounts is that the Resurrected Jesus is not recognized at first. Is this because the Resurrected Jesus comes in disguise and is deliberately hiding? Is it because the beholder is unable to recognize him? The Resurrected Jesus is present everywhere. What is needed is for the doors of our perception to be opened. We have eyes to see, ears to hear, hearts to feel, and consciousness to be raised. Our total being needs to come into new awareness.

Resurrection stories are part of the process. They serve the purpose of alerting us to some of the many possibilities of experiencing the Resurrected Jesus. In this chapter I have grouped several stories describing encounters with the Resurrected Jesus in a wide variety of ways.

Paul Meets the Resurrected Jesus as a Little Child

In *The Apocalypse of Paul*, from the Nag Hammadi Library, Paul meets a child along the road and asks directions: "By which road shall I go up to Jerusalem?" The little child replied, saying, "Say your name, so that I may show you the road" (Apocalypse of Paul 18:5-8, NHL).

After Paul gives his name, the little child says:

"I know who you are, Paul. You are he who was blessed from his mother's womb. For I have come to you that you may go up to Jerusalem to your fellow apostles. And for this reason you were called. And I am the Spirit who accompanies you. . . .

"Let your mind awaken, Paul, and see that this mountain upon which you are standing is the mountain of Jericho, so that you may know the hidden things in those that are visible. Now it is to the twelve apostles that you shall go, for they are elect spirits, and they will greet you."

(Apocalypse of Paul 18:4ff, NHL)

71

Dante's Paradisio

Paul raises his eyes and sees them greeting him.

The story continues as the child points out that Paul is already standing on a high mountain. From here Paul launches into each of the heavens, learning what he needs to know at each level until he reaches the highest heaven, which is the tenth. It is the child and the Spirit who guide Paul into this new awareness.

The story reminds us of the function of the child in our spiritual life: "And a little child shall lead them" (Isa. 11:6, NRSV).

Jesus says, "The person old in days won't hesitate to ask a child seven days old about the place of life, and that person will live" (Gospel of Thomas 4, SV). "Unless you change and become like children, you will never enter the kingdom of heaven" (Matt. 18:3, NRSV).

The Wisdom of the Resurrected Jesus is offered in many forms. Here in this story Paul discovers Wisdom from a little child. Remember, Paul was well educated in his time, well respected by serious scholars. And who is Paul's teacher? The teacher is a child.

With all due credit to Paul, notice that the process of awareness begins when he stops to ask directions. A key phrase in the story, it seems to me, is "Let your mind awaken!" His mind is very much awakened and is carried into the heavens. *"Tell me your name!"*

In one of his letters Paul writes: "I know a person in Christ who fourteen years ago was caught up to the third heaven—whether in the body or out of the body I do not know; God knows. And I know that such a person—whether in the body or out of the body I do not know; God knows—was caught up into Paradise and heard things that are not to be told, that no mortal is permitted to repeat" (2 Cor. 12:2–4, NRSV).

From the context of his letter it is clear that Paul is referring to his own experience. His letter speaks of the third heaven. The story from *The Apocalypse of Paul* speaks of the tenth heaven.[1] *See notes, p. 151*

Jesus reminds us that the Kingdom of Heaven is within us. And what launches us into the farthest reaches of inner space? In these stories of the Resurrected Jesus we discover that the launch might very well begin in a most unlikely way, like being in touch with a child or the child within us.

The Resurrected Jesus Appears as a Youth, an Old Man, and a Servant

Another resurrection experience builds and expands on the one we have just been pondering. It is found in a second-century document known as *The Apocryphon of John.*

Secrets

It happened one day when John, the brother of James—who are the sons of Zebedee—went up and came to the temple, that a Pharisee named Arimanius approached him and said to him, "Where is your master whom you followed?" And he said to him, "He has gone to the place from which he came." The Pharisee said to him, "This Nazarene deceived you with deception, and he filled your ears with lies and closed your hearts and turned you from the traditions of your fathers."

When I, John, heard these things, I turned away from the temple to a desert place, and I became greatly grieved and said in my heart, "How then was the savior chosen, and why was he sent into the world by his Father, and who is his Father who sent him, and of what sort is that aeon to which we shall go? . . ."

Straightway, while I was contemplating these things, behold the heavens opened and the whole creation which is under heaven shone and the world was shaken. And I was afraid, and behold I saw in the light a youth who stood by me. While I looked at him he became like an old man. And he changed his form again, becoming like a servant. There was not a plurality before me, but there was a likeness with multiple forms in the light, and the forms appeared through each other, and the likeness had three forms.

He said to me, "John, John, why do you doubt, and why are you afraid? You are not unfamiliar with this likeness, are you? That is to say, be not timid! I am the one who is with you for ever. I am the Father, I am the Mother, I am the Son. I am the unpolluted and incorruptible one. Now I have come to teach you what is and what was and what will come to pass, that you may know the things which are not revealed and the things which are revealed, and to teach you about the perfect Man. Now, then, lift up your face, that you may receive the things that I shall tell you today, and that you may tell them to your fellow spirits who are from the unwavering race of the perfect Man"

(Apocryphon of John 1:5–2:25, 30–32, 2:1–25, NHL).

When John goes to the Temple, tension occurs between him and the Pharisee, who feels that Jesus the Nazarene has been turning people away from the traditions. As a result of the conflict, John does not experience the Resurrected Jesus in the Temple, but rather in the desert where the heavens open. John has eyes to see the Resurrected Jesus, who changes form right before his eyes: from a youth to an old man and then to a servant.

Once again the awareness is in the eye of the beholder who is learning to see the Risen One in all the stages of life and also in the form of a servant.

Jesus is a prime example of an authentic human being who lives the life of a servant, not of a ruler. In the wilderness, Jesus said "No" to the temptation to rule over all the kingdoms of the earth. His attitude of serving continues here in this Resurrection experience.

How different this is from the attitude of those who would make the Resurrected Jesus to be a king. Once Christ is made a king, the groundwork is laid for that king to authorize a church to rule on earth, using whatever powers are needed to enforce that rule. The results are seen in the dark side of the church aligned with oppressive forces. The bloody chapters in church history occur whenever the notion of king overpowers the function of servant.

The Apocryphon of John expands the meaning of the closing phrase of Matthew's Gospel, "I AM with you always" (Matt. 28:20, NRSV). The phrase is deeply rooted in the experience of Moses when he is encountered by the Divine Mystery speaking to him from the burning bush. Moses asks, "What is your name?" The response is, "I AM that I AM." The Holy Name in Hebrew has four letters: "yod," "he," "vav," and "he." "Yod" is masculine; "he" is feminine. From these two proceed "vav," a son, and twin sister, another "he."[2]

Well-rooted in the deep meaning of the Holy Name, *The Apocryphon of John* reveals, "I AM the Father, I AM the Mother, I AM the Son. I AM the undefiled and incorruptible one." This concept reveals the wondrous Mystery as being essentially a Quaternity. The Mother, the feminine element, is missing from the trinitarian concept of "Father, Son, and Holy Spirit." The Quaternity, inherent in the Holy Name experienced by Moses, is restored here in this resurrection experience of John.

The missing feminine element is continually ignored, pushed aside, and abandoned in patriarchal religion. But in Jesus and in the resurrection experiences, the fullness of the Divine Mystery is present for all who have eyes to see. Jesus is quoted as saying, "I shall give you what no eye has seen and what no ear has heard and what no hand has touched and what has never occurred to the human mind" (Gospel of Thomas 17, NHL). During his lifetime, Jesus lived this fullness for everyone to see. Since his death and resurrection, the Risen One reveals the fullness of the Mystery in an ever widening diversity of expression.

Because of recent discoveries, we now have an expanded database on Jesus, his teachings, and also on the experiences of the Resurrected Jesus. These documents are but a sample of the variety of ways in which the Risen One is living and working in the world. The stories accomplish their purpose when they motivate us to pay attention and notice what the Risen One is doing in the world now. The challenge to us is to discover how to do our part by cooperating with the Resurrected Jesus. + priviledge

16

Ascending into
the Heavens

Jesus is not the only person who is reported to have ascended into the heavens. According to the following stories, many others have done the same thing:

In Hinduism, for example, Krishna rose from the dead and ascended bodily into the heavens. Rama, an incarnation of Vishnu after his manifestation on earth, ascended into heaven. Buddha also ascended to the celestial regions when his mission on earth was fulfilled, and marks on the rocks of a high mountain are shown and believed to be the last impression of his footsteps on earth.[1]

In the Hebrew tradition, one of the most important ascension stories is the one about the prophet Elijah, which provides the details and pattern for the ascension of Jesus. According to the story, the time has come for Elijah to die, and his successor, Elisha, is being prepared to take over. Naturally, Elisha feels he needs power from Elijah so he can do his own prophetic work effectively. He even asks for a "double portion" of Elijah's spirit. Elijah agrees that this will happen, provided Elisha pays attention and sees him going into heaven.

The day arrives, and so does a fiery chariot with horses to pick up Elijah. As Elijah soars off into the heavens, Elisha catches sight of him and says, "My Father. . . ." Elijah drops his mantle to the ground and Elisha catches it; now he has the symbol of prophetic power. Elisha goes down to the Jordan wearing this mantle, the cloak that wraps him in power. Elisha removes his mantle and uses it to strike the water, which immediately parts in two. Just as Moses parted the waters of the Red Sea with his staff, now Elisha parts the waters of the Jordan with his mantle.

When it is time for Jesus to ascend into heaven, he takes his closest disciples to the edge of town, where he tells them to wait in Jerusalem until they receive power from on high. Jesus says his good-byes, shares the Peace with them and ascends out of sight. He does not drop his mantle, but ten days later he drops his Spirit on them with tremendous power. Those who saw Jesus go into the heavens receive even more than a double portion of his power through the outpouring of the Holy Spirit.

You can go to Jerusalem today and visit the site on the Mount of Olives where Jesus is said to have ascended into the heavens, leaving his footprint in the solid rock.

From the Mount of Olives you get a magnificent view of the Dome of the Rock. Tradition says that this is the rock where Isaac was about to sacrifice his son Jacob when an angel suggested that sacrificing a ram might be a better idea. Over the centuries, countless other animals have been sacrificed on that site. Because it is such a holy place, it provided a great location for the prophet Muhammad to ascend into heaven, which is what he is reported to have done in 632 C.E. His followers erected the beautiful mosque with a gold dome over the rock.

There is a a great deal of humor inherent in the ascension stories that serves as a vehicle that helps carry their inherent truth. Holy Scripture has a habit of telling outrageous stories so that once you hear them you are not likely to forget them. Once you get the story in mind and are paying attention, then you can ask questions like "What in the world does it mean?" and "What difference can it possibly make in our lives?"

You are free to decide whether or not you accept the ascension of Jesus or any of the ascension stories as literal historic fact. But I will affirm here as strongly as I can that these stories, like the virgin birth stories, are very true symbolically.

I invite you to consider two of my favorite ascension stories, one from *The Secret Letter of James* and the other from The Gospel of Peter.

Ascension as Related by The Secret Book of James

As we have seen, *The Secret Book of James* is an experience of the Resurrected Jesus who continues teaching the disciples by taking aside two people, James and Peter. The book concludes with a story of the Resurrected Jesus ascending into heaven with these final parting words: "Now I shall ascend to the place from which I have come. But you, when I was eager to go, have rebuffed me; instead of accompanying me, you have chased me away" (Secret Book of James 9:7–8, SV).

As you may recall, the original rebuff was when the disciples had complained by saying, "You went away and left us!" That remark must have hurt and stung a bit, because at the close of his teaching session, the Risen One remembers it and speaks about it.

Having gotten that off his chest, the Resurrected Jesus continues: "Still, pay attention to the glory that awaits me and, having opened your hearts, listen to the hymns that await me up in heaven. For today I must take my place at the right hand of the Father. I have spoken my last word to you. For a chariot of spirit has lifted me up, and from now on I shall strip myself so that I may clothe myself" (Secret Book of James 9:9–11, SV).

The phrase "I shall strip myself so that I may clothe myself" has several layers of meaning. The first layer is a reference back to the baptism of Jesus. Normally, anyone being baptized would first remove all clothing.

Status and function are defined quickly by uniforms for nurses, soldiers, prisoners, priests, and a host of others who wear special clothing when they are "on duty." Likewise, executives, business people, persons hoping to attract mates, and most all of us use clothing to define who we are and help accomplish what we want to attain. We can either use clothing as an outer expression of how we feel inside, or we can fall prey to the clothing advertising that is designed to try to make us believe that we can become what we want by starting with a new wardrobe. These are a few of the things that come to mind regarding the functions of clothing.

Now what happens when we take all that away? It is one thing to remove one's clothing in private when taking a shower or making love. But what might happen if we were to remove all clothing in public?

In the Garden of Eden, "The man and his wife were both naked, and were not ashamed" (Gen. 2:25, NRSV). Recalling the Creation story and speaking from his own baptism experience, Jesus teaches that "when you strip without being ashamed, and you take your clothes and put them under your feet like little children and trample on them, then will you see the son of the living one, and you will not be afraid" (Gospel of Thomas 37, SV).

Jesus, in his baptism in the Jordan, voluntarily strips himself, preparing to be clothed with the Holy Spirit. Then he teaches his disciples what this action can mean. Now he declares clearly that once again "I shall strip myself so that I may clothe myself."

Notice also how this stripping himself resembles the ascension story of Elijah who removes his mantle and lets it drop from his chariot as he soars into the heavens. He lets it fall so that Elisha, his successor, may pick it up. The power that clothed Elijah is now available to clothe Elisha. Likewise, Jesus will strip himself, leaving his clothing behind, so that he may reclothe himself in the garments of glory. In other words, Jesus drops his physical body in order to become embodied in his family, friends, and followers. They, in turn, have the potential of being transformed into the glorified Body of Christ, his Heavenly Bride (Revelation 18–22).

Elijah leaves in a chariot of fire. Jesus leaves in a chariot of Spirit. These are two ways of saying the same thing because fire is a symbol of the Spirit. The intense energy of the Spirit makes the blastoff of a rocket mere child's play.

Having told James and Peter what was about to happen, the Risen One tells them to stay alert, "So pay attention: congratulations to those who proclaimed the Son before he descended, so that, having come, I might ascend. Congratulations three times over to those who were proclaimed by the Son before they existed, so that you might have a share with them" (Secret Book of James 9:12–13, SV).

I smile when I read the words, "Pay attention" because they resonate so clearly with the essential teachings of the Dalai Lama, Thich Nhat Hanh, the Buddhist monk, and so many other authentic spiritual teachers.

After saying "Pay attention," he goes away. James and Peter kneel down, give thanks, and send their hearts up to heaven. They hear with their ears and see with their eyes the sound of battles, a trumpet's blast, and utter turmoil. James tells us:

> When we passed beyond that place, we sent our minds up further. We saw with our eyes and heard with our ears hymns and angelic praises and angelic rejoicing.
>
> After this, we all desired to send our spirits heavenward to the majesty. And when we went up, we were not permitted to see or hear a thing for the rest of the disciples called to us and asked us, "What did you hear from the Teacher?" and "What did he tell you?" and "Where has he gone?"
>
> We answered them, "He has ascended. He has given us a pledge and promised all of us life, and disclosed to us children who are to come after us, having bid us to love them, since we will be saved for their sake."
>
> (Secret Book of James 9:7–10:9, SV).

Ascension as Envisioned in The Gospel of Peter

In *The Gospel of Peter,* resurrection and ascension are essentially one event:

> "Early at first light on the sabbath, a crowd came from Jerusalem to see the sealed tomb. But during the night before the Lord's day dawned, while the soldiers were on guard, two by two during each watch, a loud noise came from the sky, and they saw the skies open up and two men come down from there in a burst of light and approach the tomb. The stone that had been pushed against the entrance began to roll away by itself and moved away to one side; then the tomb opened up and both young men went inside.
>
> Now when the soldiers saw this, they roused the centurion from his sleep, along with the elders. (Remember, they were also there keeping watch.) While they were explaining what they had seen, again

they see three men leaving the tomb, two supporting the third, and a cross following them. The heads of the two reached up to the sky, while the head of the third, whom they had led by the hand, reached beyond the skies. And they heard a voice from the skies that said, "Have you preached to those who sleep?" And an answer was heard from the cross: "Yes!"

(Gospel of Peter 9:1–11:7, SV)

Who are the two men who come for Jesus? These are the same two who appear in the story of the transfiguration, Moses and Elijah, who represent the Law and the Prophets. These two return for Jesus after he dies and take him with them to heaven. Thus, one of the meanings embodied in the transfiguration story is being reinforced here in this ascension story. The gospel of Christ brings together the best of Law and Prophets and shows them in a new light that outshines everything that came before.

Consider the meaning of the cross following along behind Elijah, Moses, and Jesus. Before the crucifixion, Jesus had to carry the cross; now it is moving on its own energy. Furthermore, the cross now has the ability to speak. Would anyone in right mind believe this happened? At the literal level it is preposterous. But at the mythic level it is very true. The cross has a great power of its own and a message of its own that all the preachers in all of time are unable to exhaust. Yet the message of the cross can be profoundly simple as it is in this story. When asked, "Have you preached to those who sleep?" the simple one-word answer from the cross is "Yes!"

What might be the message as told from the point of view of the cross itself? If you yourself were the cross, what would it be like for you to be the one to bear the innocent, tortured, writhing body of Jesus until he breathed his last breath, slumped on you, and died? What might it have felt like for you as the cross to feel the nails being pulled out of you, to watch the body being laid on the ground? How would you feel as Mother Earth begins shaking and quaking in her agony? Suppose you are the cross following along after the bearers of the body into the tomb where you wait to see what might happen next? Imagine you are the cross watching Elijah and Moses entering the tomb, waking Jesus from his cruel sleep. As the three of them start walking out of the tomb and gently rise into space, wouldn't you want to go along with them? And if someone asks you a question, might you have something to say?

Now that we have a bit more of the feeling of the story, let us explore some of its deeper meaning. The cross preaches to "those who sleep." Who might they be? One interpretation says that these are the dead who lived before the time of Jesus. If so, where do they reside? Are they in graves and tombs? How do they hear the message from the cross? Visions of bodies coming out of graves provide material for horror movies, but do we believe these things as actual events?

Another interpretation would be to recognize that those who have died live not in the graves of cemeteries, but in the collective unconscious that is transmitted from generation to generation and dwells within the depths of every human being. The church affirms faith in the communion of saints in which all the faithful of the past are accessible to us now. Biological studies reveal that information is transmitted from generation to generation through the DNA. Eastern thought describes a process of reincarnation. All four concepts are attempting to describe the mysterious continuity connecting all generations. Each concept has a particular perspective and uses its own descriptive vocabulary. All four approaches converge in one mysterious reality whose heart is the message of the cross.

Yet another understanding of the cross preaching to "those who sleep" might be a reference to those who are alive but are only sleepwalking through life. They are apathetic, disengaged, not involved in really living. Might the message of the cross be quite powerful in waking up the sleepwalkers?

This rich resurrection-ascension story from *The Gospel of Peter* invites us to meditate freshly on the meaning and power of these mysterious events. Those whose minds are fixed in literal thinking may have trouble with these stories. But those who are discovering how to live mythically will find their lives enriched beyond measure. Once the chains of literalism are broken, the true myths will set us free.

The mythic material in the stories of the baptism, life, death, burial, resurrection, and ascension of Jesus expresses itself through the hearts and minds of the family, friends, and followers of Jesus and their communities. Because the material is archetypal, it persists in our individual souls and collective psyche.

Dark Forces Fuel Resurrection and Ascension

As another example of meditating on the meaning of the cross, consider a mythic account of the crucifixion of St. Andrew, who meditates on the death of Jesus while facing his own. His meditation is from the second-century *Acts of Andrew*:

> Andrew came to the place where he was to be crucified. And when he saw the cross set in the sand at the seashore he left them all and went to the cross and with a strong voice addressed it as if it were a living creature:
>
> "Hail, O Cross; indeed may you rejoice. I know well that you will rest in the future because for a long time you have been weary set up waiting for me. I am coming to you whom I recognize as mine own;

I am coming to you, who long for me. I know the mystery for which you have been set up. For you are set up in the cosmos to establish the unstable.

"And one part of you stretches up to heaven so that you may point out the heavenly Logos (Tao) the head of all things. Another part of you is stretched out to right and left that you may put to flight the fearful inimical power and draw the cosmos to unity. And another part of you is set on the earth, rooted in the depths, that you may bring what is on earth and under the earth into contact with what is in heaven.

"O Cross, tool of salvation of the Most High! O Cross, trophy of the victory of Christ over his enemies! O Cross, planted on earth and bearing your fruit in heaven! O name of the Cross, filled with all things!

"Well done, form of understanding, that you have given a form to your own formlessness! Well done, invisible discipline, that you discipline severely the substance of the knowledge of many gods and drive out from humanity its discoverer! Well done, O Cross, that you have clothed yourself with the Lord, and borne as fruit and robber, and called the apostle to repentance, and not thought it beneath you to receive us!

"But for how long shall I say these things and not be embraced by the Cross, that in the Cross I may be made to live and through the Cross I may go out of this life into the common death? Approach, ministers of my joy and servants of Aegeates, and fulfill the desire we both have and bind the lamb to the suffering, the man to the Creator, the soul to the Saviour."

The blessed Andrew said this standing on the ground and staring steadfastly towards the cross. Then he besought the brethren that the executioners should come and carry out what they had been commanded. For they were standing at a distance.

And they came and bound his hands and his feet and did not nail him; for they had been so instructed by Aegeates. He wished in this way to torture him as he hung in that he would be eaten alive by dogs. And they left him hanging and departed from him.

And when the crowds that stood around who had been made disciples in Christ by him saw that they did none of these things which were usual in the case of crucifixions, they hoped to hear again something from him. For as he hung he moved his head and smiled.[2]

This chapter is about the ascension. My purpose in drawing attention to the cross is a simple one and can be posed in the form of a question: Where did the energy for ascending originate? In a word, I believe the answer is "the cross."

might explain the wisdom in trees

All the dark forces of human and cosmic existence converge in the arche-
type of crucifixion, which is why suffering people in countless situations have
drawn inspiration and strength to bear their own pain. In the crucifixion "the
powers of hell have done their worst." And that is not the end of the story
because out of suffering new life may emerge.

Put it another way: Just as rocket fuel provides power for a spaceship to
blast off into space, so the cross provides the energy for resurrection and ascension. We all know that plants, dinosaurs, and all the other animals who lived
and died have been transformed into the rocket fuel that blasts spaceships out
into space. In a very real sense, they all died to set us free!

And while these plants and animals were living, where did they draw their
energy? All energy, all life on earth, and even this planet itself originated in the
sun. In a very real sense, a spaceship moving toward the sun is powered by
energy that originated there!

In like manner, the dark powers that produced the cross also provide the
fuel for resurrection and ascension, returning us to the source from which we
all originate.

Now consider where this cycle of death and resurrection occurs. Is it a
one-time occurrence of one person in the first century? Or might the cycle
embodied in Jesus be the recurring paradigm for our time and all time?

The cycles of death, burial, resurrection, and ascension are being lived out
within the depths of our own being and within human communities, both
local and global.

17

Sharing Resurrection Through Writing and Singing

Imagine that you are one of the friends or followers of Jesus living in one of the villages in Galilee. You are about the same age as Jesus. You might have known him before he met John. Imagine that you are there on the day when John is baptizing Jesus. You see Jesus go down into the water and then notice the smile on his face as he comes up laughing (Gospel of Philip 74:29). Then you see Jesus wander off and disappear into the wilderness. What in the world is going on?

When Jesus returns from the wilderness, you notice changes in him, especially his new passion for teaching. Jesus seems to have something important to say. You pay close attention and listen carefully. Jesus fascinates you, and you make it a point to be present to hear what he has to say. You ponder the questions he raises and ask a few questions yourself.

Jesus moves along to other villages to teach. Both he and his disciples urge you to travel with them. Are you ready to leave each time he says, "We're on the road again"?

Suppose you have work to do and a family to take care of, so you choose to stay put in your own Galilean village and catch Jesus every time he comes through town. Furthermore, you reason that if what he says makes sense, then it ought to work right where you are in your own ordinary context. You take heart when Jesus agrees with you.

So you stay where you are. Jesus goes away for a while, yet his teachings keep working on you from inside. You are beginning to get in touch with the Kingdom of God within you. You are experiencing the seed of true humanity breaking open and sprouting within. You are beginning to feel more and more like an authentic human being. Something very real is coming alive in you. You feel yourself changing in refreshing ways.

Imagine that you, like Jesus, are Jewish and meet regularly with the local congregation wherever they get together in the center of town. You and the others in your congregation don't need a building to meet in; gathering near the well in the center of town works just fine.

Two or three years pass, and you are making mental note of more and more of the teachings of Jesus. The things he says stick with you. His stories are memorable, and his one-liners fix themselves in your memory. You talk about them with your friends. Sometimes you find yourself involved in hot debates over whether his teaching is something entirely new or is a deeper understanding of the traditions you were taught as a child.

Then comes that fateful day. Jesus has been teaching in your village, and now he announces his plans to go up to Jerusalem for Passover. He, like many other people in your village, has been going to Jerusalem for the major festivals just about every year.

You are concerned and a bit worried because you know that when everybody crowds into the city things get rather crazy. There is too much noise and too much activity. It is hard to find a place to stay, and the merchants usually jack up the prices. Besides, there is a great deal of unrest and fights often break out. Who needs the hassle? Furthermore, Jesus has become more and more controversial, and there just might be big trouble for him if he goes into Jerusalem.

You overhear Peter trying to persuade Jesus to stay in Galilee and not go into the city this time. It is too risky. Jesus gets hot under the collar, swears at Peter, and says, "Get behind me Satan!" Jesus can be hard to deal with when he has already made up his mind about what he is going to do! Peter yields to Jesus and goes to Jerusalem with him. So does Mary Magdalene, Joanna, most of the women, and quite a number of the other disciples.

But you know the idea is crazy and just too risky. So you and a number of the other disciples stay right where you are in Galilee. Naturally, you are concerned about Jesus and what might happen to him. You keep in touch through people going back and forth to the city.

Before long you and everyone else who remains in Galilee are shocked and stunned to hear that Jesus has been arrested, pushed through quick trials, and executed. Before he went to Jerusalem you felt it might be bad, but you didn't know it would end with Jesus' being given the death penalty.

You feel like saying, "I warned him not to go there." But what good would that do? What has happened has happened. Jesus is dead. Is this the end of everything?

You remain where you are and definitely stay clear of Jerusalem. The authorities may very well start rounding up his friends. You need to share your grief, so you talk with the other disciples who, like yourself, remained in Galilee.

On the Sabbath you meet with the rest of the congregation for the usual reading and teaching from the Holy Scriptures. You join in chanting the psalms and offering prayers. It gets a little tense sometimes because in the congregation are not only the friends and disciples of Jesus but also his opponents.

The next day, Sunday, you meet with the friends of Jesus. A strange thing happens. Just about every time you meet, you have the feeling that Jesus is still with you. People are saying, "I have seen the Lord!" Jesus has risen from the dead. You know this is true because you feel it.

You notice how much Jesus is with you as you and the others reminisce about him. People are remembering the things that Jesus said:

"The Kingdom of Heaven is within you"; "You are the light of the world"; You are salt of the earth"; "When someone strikes you on the cheek, offer the other as well."

Others chime in, "Yes, and how about his stories: the one on journey, the father with two sons, the woman baking bread, and all the others?" Someone else with a sense of humor adds, "And don't forget his camel jokes!"

Collecting the Teachings of Jesus—*The Q Gospel*

Time passes. It has been about twenty years since Jesus was crucified. People who knew Jesus personally are getting older; many have died. You are feeling that the time has come to write down his teachings. You consider yourself a competent writer, but you need some help in remembering. You decide to gather some other people together to make a collection of the teachings of Jesus.

Little do you know that in another twenty years other writers will take what you have written, expand it with information about his healing ministry, and add stories about Jesus' last days in Jerusalem. You knew those things had happened, but you hadn't actually witnessed them. Besides, you simply wanted to write about what you knew best—his teachings. This document will be your contribution; others can add to it later if they have more recollections.

I have asked you to imagine this scenario because apparently something like that happened in the creation of a document now known as the Lost Gospel of Q, which may very well have originated in Galilee. "Q" might seem like a strange name for a Gospel. It stands for "Quelle," the German word for "Source." German scholars were the first to identify and name this source Gospel.

The Q Gospel begins with a brief account of Jesus' Baptism and continues with a collection of sayings attributed to him. There are two healing stories, but otherwise no accounts about Jesus' life, death, or resurrection.

The Gospels of Matthew and Luke build their stories on the Gospel of Mark. They also contain almost identical passages not found in Mark. Scholars are quite certain that these passages are from *The Q Gospel*.[1]

The Thomas Community Writes a Gospel

Friends and followers of Jesus who had known him before his crucifixion continue to meet together, remember him, and in most instances experience his continuing presence with them. His body is being re-membered; the members of his body of followers are becoming the Body of Christ.

Oral traditions develop wherever there are people who recollect and keep on talking. Those of us living in the twenty-first century who want information on Jesus and the early communities of Christ are indebted to those who took the time and trouble to re-collect, re-member, and re-create their experiences in writing.

The earliest written documents about Jesus are collections of his teachings. The most important of these are *The Q Gospel* and *The Gospel of Thomas*. The first editions of both were written about 50 C.E., but in different locations. It is likely that *Q* originated back home in Galilee and *Thomas* was written in Syria, with a little help from folks in Galilee.[2]

In both situations, the process is much the same. Time is passing. Those who knew Jesus are getting older, and many have died. It becomes clear to those who are living in the Spirit of the Resurrected Jesus that the teachings should be preserved through writing.

Thomas is a wonderful Gospel that has parallels with *Q* plus sayings attributed to Jesus that are found nowhere else.

For example:

> Jesus said, "If those who lead you say to you, 'See the Kingdom is in the sky,' then the birds of the sky will precede you. If they say to you, 'It is in the sea,' then the fish will precede you. Rather, the Kingdom is inside of you, and it is outside of you. When you come to know yourselves, then you will become known, and you will realize that it is you who are the sons of the living Father. But if you will not know yourselves, you dwell in poverty and it is you who are that poverty"
> (Gospel of Thomas 3, NHL).

Over and over again, Jesus gives us teachings that we can use on our own instead of expecting him to do it for us. He shows us the Way, and we do the walking. Jesus said to his disciples:

> "Compare me to someone and tell Me whom I am like."
> Simon Peter said to Him, "You are like a righteous angel."
> Matthew said to Him, "You are like a wise philosopher."
> Thomas said to Him, "Master, my mouth is wholly incapable of saying whom You are like."

Jesus said, "I am not your master. Because you have drunk, you have become intoxicated from the bubbling spring which I have measured out."

(Gospel of Thomas 13, NHL)

Does it seems startling for Jesus to say, "I am *not* your Master"? The usual master-servant relationship is clear. Masters issue orders and their servants obey. Servants have little or no responsibility for making decisions; they simply do as they are told. Jesus does not want that kind of relationship with us. His function in our lives is to provide us with tools for us to take and use in our own lives.

A specific example of this is a scene with two brothers who have been arguing over an inheritance issue. One of the brothers comes to Jesus and says, "Tell my brother to divide the family inheritance with me." But Jesus says, "Friend, who set me to be a judge or arbitrator over you?" (Luke 12:13–14, NRSV). Jesus calls the man "Friend," so clearly he is speaking to him with warmth and caring. He is also making it clear that the brothers should solve their problem themselves. If they have been paying attention to the teachings of Jesus, they may discover some clues that will help them work things out.

One teaching in particular that might be useful is the one where Jesus says, "Love your brother like your soul, guard him like the pupil of your eye." Eyesight being so precious, we naturally give great care to our eyes to prevent their being injured in any way. Jesus is clear about the same kind of caring in a relationship. Then he goes into the dynamics of the relationship. In the next sentence Jesus says: "You see the sliver in your brother's eye, but you do not see the timber in your own eye. When you cast the sliver out of your own eye, then you will see clearly to cast the timber out of your brother's eye" (Matt. 7:3, SV).

Today, we might identify the dynamic as one of projection. Like the projector in a movie theater sending images to a screen, so we often project unconscious parts of ourselves onto others.

When another person seems especially irritating, we might identify what it is that bothers us, then pause and ask, "Is there anything like that in me?" What we think we see in another may very well be something we need to deal with in ourselves. Once we have examined our own projections, then we are able to see the other person more clearly.

There are negative projections in which our own dark side is projected onto others. There are also strong positive projections where we see something we think is so wonderful in another person. The joy of working with our positive projections is to discover that this positive quality is also within us. We need to get in touch with it and express it as well.

Consistently, Jesus points us to the life within, to the inner dynamics that require our attention if we are to live fully. The Resurrected Jesus seeks to continue with us the same kind of relationships that Jesus had with his friends, disciples, and even his opponents.

Ironically, much of religious teaching would expect people to become servants to the Master. The message seems to be: obey Christ as the Judge. Whenever obedience is the dominant message, then we depart from Jesus who says, "I am *not* your Master."

Jesus shows us the patterns, the Way, so that we can walk in it and take our own responsibilities. When we are living in the Spirit of Jesus, responsibility translates into "the ability to repose."

The Gospel of Thomas has a number of memorable one-liners like this one:

"If they ask you, 'What is the sign of your Father in you?' say to them, 'It is movement and response'" (Gospel of Thomas 50, NHL).

Can you feel that sense of moving and resting? Music is based on finding the rhythm of movement and rest. Likewise, our lives are designed to be lived rhythmically. Essentially, life is a dance set to music. We need to find the rhythm, the pattern, the pacing. If ever there were a teaching that is needed for our overly fast-paced society, it is this one.

Resurrection Expressed Through Singing New Songs

Speaking of music, some of the people who encountered the Resurrected Jesus expressed their feelings in song.

Have you ever wondered what the family and friends of Jesus sang when they met together in the days, weeks, months, and years following his death? Most of his original disciples were Jews, so their repertoire would have begun with the familiar collection of songs known as *The Book of Psalms*.

Their experiences needed fresh expression, so they began singing new songs. After a while, they took some of the oral singing tradition and began writing the words down. Unfortunately, musical notation hadn't been invented yet, so we have the words without the tunes. One of the priceless gifts to us is a collection of songs known as *The Odes of Solomon* written ca. 100 C.E.

King Solomon, reigning 976–936 B.C.E., lived a thousand years before *The Odes of Solomon* were written. Because he could not possibly have written them, why is Solomon's name attached to this collection of songs?

Solomon was already associated with the delightful erotic poetry called *The Song of Solomon*. His father, King David, was associated with *The Book of Psalms*. New music being composed gained more immediate acceptance when it was associated with the tradition of David and Solomon.

The situation is rather like Old King Cole, that merry old soul who called for his pipe, called for his bowl, and called for his fiddlers three. We remember

King Cole, but who knows the names of his fiddlers? So who were the people who wrote the songs in the collection known as *The Odes of Solomon*? We know they belonged to an early community of Christ, but their names are lost forever.

In a very real sense, the One who deserves the most credit for composition is the Spirit of the living Christ, who touches hearts and sets them free to express musically what they are feeling. There are forty-two *Odes*. The second one is missing, but we have all the others in a fresh translation, thanks to Willis Barnstone. The following are a few samples of odes:

"As the wind moves over the harp and the strings speak
    so your Spirit sings through all parts of my body . . .
    and I sing through your love . . . "

Ode 6

Remember the song "Play Me"? Will you imagine yourself as the harp and allow the Spirit of God to play you?

The odes are warm and personal songs like these:

"Open your ears
    and I will speak to you.
Give me your soul
    that I may give you mine . . ."

Ode 9

"The Lord has changed my mouth by his word
    and opened my heart by his light . . ."

Ode 10

"Look, the Lord is our mirror.
    Open your eyes and see your eyes in him . . . ."

Ode 13

"As the sun is joy to those who seek daybreak,
    so my joy is the Lord . . ."

Ode 15

"I was rescued from my chains
    and fled to you my God . . ."

Ode 30

Anyone who has been freed from addiction can put heart into lines like these!

Tucked inside the odes are lines like these:

"Love me tenderly
     you who love . . ."

Ode 8:12

And in another we find these lines:

"Let singers sing the grace of the Lord most high,
     let them sing.
Let their hearts be like day,
     their harmonies like the Lord's excellent beauty . . ."

Ode 7

The first-century family and friends of Jesus who took the time to write about their experiences of Jesus and the Resurrected Jesus have given us priceless gifts. Among the first to put pen to parchment were the people of the Q community in Galilee and the Thomas community in Syria. Other writers built on their work along with their own spirit-filled experiences. Today the Jesus Seminar Scholars have collected and arranged *The Complete Gospels*, the most comprehensive collection of Gospel material available to date.

Special thanks go to the musicians and singers who allowed the Spirit of the Resurrected Jesus to be released through them in song. The anonymous scribes who took the time to record the lyrics deserve very honorable mention. I often wish their music had been recorded for us so we could play it and hear the chants and melodies as well. Even though the people of the first century did not have recording technology available to them, the same Spirit they knew is available to sing these spiritually delightful words through us in the musical idioms of our time.

One thing is certain: the same Spirit who was being released through them still resides in our souls ready for expression through us and the sounds of our time. Being someone who resonates with the blues, I wonder what some of the words of *The Odes of Solomon* might feel like when set to B.B. King tunes.

Music has always been an integral part of renewal movements. The *Odes* gave expression in the early centuries. Psalms set to plainsong provided the moods for the monastic movement. Hymns carried the sixteenth-century Protestant Reformation forward. Gospel songs empower twentieth-century Evangelical and Pentecostal movements. New Age folks move into new spaces with their ambient sounds.

What musical sounds will enliven the most genuine spiritual expressions of our twenty-first century? Music tends to be cumulative over time, so many of the sounds from earlier centuries may continue to be part of our musical repertoire. In addition, might new sounds be emerging?

I suspect the twenty-first century will mirror the diversity of the first century. I imagine there will be a variety of resurrection experiences and a full range of heartfelt musical expressions. What will the new music sound like? Meanwhile, I will chant and sing whatever way the Spirit impels me. If we all do that as individuals and in communities, what joys may come!

"Open your hearts to the exultation of the Lord
    and flow your love from your heart to your lips in holy life"

Ode 8

18

Bread Rising in
Eucharistic Communities

From the wealth of evidence, it is clear that shortly after the death of Jesus many members of his family and friends gather and begin experiencing a Real Presence within, around, and beyond them. In addition, another profound reality is beginning to be felt. As people assemble in the name of Jesus, they discover that they themselves are becoming members of a living body that is soon identified and named as the Body of Christ.

Passover Seder Evolves into Eucharist

When they meet, pray, and share a meal together, they discover that the Resurrected Jesus is among them. Shared holy meals have already been part of the common life for the Jewish followers of Jesus. The Passover Meal known as the Seder has always carried great meaning as a celebration of freedom.

The ceremonial foods are an integral part in conveying the meaning of the Exodus story. Spring greens are dipped into salt water as a reminder of the salty tears shed by people in captivity. Bitter herbs are eaten as well. Charoset, a spread resembling mortar, serves as a reminder of the bricks that the enslaved Israelites were required to make. There is always a roasted shank bone of lamb symbolizing the blood of the lamb smeared on the doorposts to remind the Angel of Death to pass them over.

During the Passover Meal the people always eat matzoth, the flat unleavened bread, a reminder that the Exodus was made in a hurry. There was no time to add yeast and let the bread rise. And of course there is wine, plenty of wine, for celebration.

The tradition of the Passover Meal serves as the original menu for eucharistic meals that members of the Body of Christ begin celebrating together. There are clear continuities between the Passover Meal and the Eucharist. Both are celebrations of freedom. Both make use of the cup of wine raised in praise and thanksgiving to the Lord of Life. Both include the sharing of holy bread.

Seder is celebrated once a year at Passover. When Seder evolves into the Eucharist, it becomes a weekly freedom celebration. Evidence is shown in *The Didache*, a first-century church manual, which provides these instructions. "On every Lord's Day—his special day—come together and break bread and give thanks" (Didache 14:1, Cyril Richardson trans.).[1]

The development of eucharistic worship follows an identifiable sequence. First comes the experience of the Resurrected Jesus during worship, which includes the reading of Scripture, deeply felt extemporaneous prayer, and joyous sharing of the eucharistic meal. Second, people tell one another what they have been experiencing while praying, singing, and celebrating eucharistic meals. Third, they begin writing down their experiences. Fourth, they collect these writings, copy them, and circulate them to other communities. Living liturgy continues to evolve and change. Over time, liturgies and prayer books are written. These, too, require a continuing process of revision.

Today the sequence is often reversed. We start with the liturgies and collections of writings, like the New Testament, that have come down to us. We pray the liturgies and study the writings, hoping to experience what the original followers of Jesus may have known.

The old documents have enormous value and point the way for our own spiritual life. The New Testament and other early writings are important because they are a means to an end—to enter into direct experience of the Resurrected Jesus now.

Stories and liturgies are packed with symbolic meaning. The symbolic helps bring us together when the demonic is seeking to drive us apart. Let's face it, much of life these days is demonic. We live with very strong forces hell bent on tearing things apart. How much easier it is to tear things down than it is to build them up. It is easier to be critical than to be constructive. Demonic forces need to be countered with symbolic ones that will bring together, reconcile, heal, and build up. There is a tremendous need for the symbolic to bring mending to our broken world.

One of the early stories is about a Last Supper that includes the instruction from Jesus, "Do this in remembrance of me." Is it because of a command that people share the Eucharist? Or is the Eucharist celebrated because followers of Jesus discover that when they meet together and break bread the Resurrected Jesus is with them? Is it a command or an experience that keeps them celebrating week by week, year by year for two thousand years?

Commands alone lose their power. Orders become hollow and meaningless unless something important is actually occurring. When there is no vitality connected with a task or ritual, people lose interest, forget, or just don't get around to it. A few obedient souls keep on doing it, but all that remains are old habits and meaningless forms. Sooner or later people ask, "Why bother?" People drift away. Communities dissipate and die.

In utter contrast, the early documents assure us that in the eucharistic gatherings something vital is really going on. The Eucharist evolved not from a command, but from the vital experience of participants. *The Didache* provides gentle symbolic meaning such as this: "Just as the grains were scattered over the hillside, and then were brought together to form one loaf of bread, so may the church be gathered together from the ends of the earth into your kingdom" (Didache 9:4).

Scattered grains is an apt description. So often our lives, families, and churches are scattered, and our institutions become dysfunctional. How we yearn to have all the pieces brought together! Where is the unity in the diversity? Where is the harmony in all the range of sounds? Where is the wholeness in a world of brokenness?

In the marriage service of the 1979 *Book of Common Prayer*, one of the prayers for the couple says, "Make their life together a sign of Christ's love to this sinful and broken world, that unity may overcome estrangement, forgiveness heal guilt, and joy conquer despair." At first it looks as though the prayer has great expectations for a couple making their commitment and starting their married life together. Actually, the primary focus is on Christ's love manifesting in actual human situations like marriages, congregations, institutions, and the usual contexts of human interaction.

The experience of the Resurrected Jesus can bring together what is broken and scattered, can heal what has been torn and dis-eased. People in the early Jesus movement experience this coming together by the power of the Holy Spirit. Then they put their experience into words as in *The Prayer of Thanksgiving*, one of the documents in the Nag Hammadi Library: "This is the prayer that they spoke, We give thanks to you! Every soul and heart is lifted up to You! . . . Give us mind, so that we may understand You, speech, so that we may expound You, knowledge so that we may know You" (Prayer of Thanksgiving, NHL).

Words like that are not invented hoping that they might happen. They are expressions of what people are actually feeling.

Like the Gospels, the earliest layers of liturgical tradition were first oral and then written. Prayers giving genuine expression to the experience began to take shape. When they evolved into written form, they could be repeated and used with greater regularity.

For example, here is the continuation of the heartfelt eucharistic prayer above:

"We rejoice, having been illumined by Your knowledge. We rejoice because You have shown us Yourself. We rejoice because while we were in the body, You have made us divine through Your knowledge.

"The thanksgiving of the one who attains to You is one thing: that we know You. We have known You, O intellectual light. O life of life, we have known You. O womb of every creature, we have known You. O womb pregnant with the nature of the Father, we have known You. O eternal permanence of the begetting Father, thus have we worshipped your goodness. There is one petition that we ask: we would be preserved in knowledge. And there is one protection that we desire: that we not stumble in this kind of life".

(Prayer of Thanksgiving, NHL)

After praying in this intense and intimate way, the assembled members of Christ's Body embraced each other and then shared their holy food.

Notice that in this prayer people are praying to both the Father and the Womb of every creature. Both the masculine and feminine aspects of the Source of Life are felt and known.

Sharing Bread and Three Cups

Some of the ceremonial foods of the Seder meal continue to be used, particularly the bread and cup of wine. Did you know that many early celebrations included four elements? *The Apostolic Tradition of Hippolytus* (ca. 217 C.E.). describes an even earlier tradition of bread and three cups:

And when the offering is immediately brought by the deacons to the bishop, and by thanksgiving he shall make the bread into an image of the body of Christ, and the cup of wine mixed with water according to the likeness of the blood, which is shed for all who believe in him.

And milk and honey mixed together for the fulfillment of the promise to the fathers, which spoke of a land flowing with milk and honey; namely, Christ's flesh which he gave, by which they who believe are nourished like babes, he making sweet the bitter things of the heart by the gentleness of his word.

And the water into an offering in a token of the laver,[1] in order that the inner part of man, which is a living soul, may receive the same as the body.

The Bishop shall explain the reason of all these things to those who partake. And when he breaks the bread and distributes the fragments he shall say: The heavenly bread in Christ Jesus. And the recipient shall say, Amen.

And the presbyters—or if there are not enough presbyters, the deacons—shall hold the cups, and shall stand by with reverence and modesty; first he who holds the water, then the milk, thirdly the wine.

And the recipients shall taste of each three times, he who gives the cup saying: In God the Father Almighty; and the recipient shall say, Amen. Then: In the Lord Jesus Christ; and he shall say, Amen. Then: In the Holy Spirit and the holy church; and he shall say, Amen. So it shall be done to each.

And when these things are completed, let each one hasten to do good works and to please God and to live aright, devoting himself to the church, practising the things he has learned, advancing in the service of God.

(Apostolic Tradition of Hippolytus 23[3])

Symbols take on life for us when we start with their literal meaning and then explore their symbolic value.

Bread is the staff of life. Bread, in all its many forms, is found everywhere. It is a basic and universal food, both literally and symbolically. For example, the Israelites in the wilderness were given manna, the bread from heaven.

Water, quite literally, is our native substance. We live the first nine months of our existence in the water of our mother's womb. We are born in water. Our bodies are more than 98 percent water plus a few chemicals. Furthermore, we cannot survive without water. Symbolically, it brings to mind all the great stories of water including Creation, the Flood, the Exodus, baptism, the Holy Spirit, and many more.

Milk and honey combined recalls our first food, the sweet milk from our mother's breasts. The Israelites were being led toward a promised land flowing with milk and honey. The Holy Scriptures often use the phrase, as in the Psalms: "How sweet are your words to my taste, sweeter than honey to my mouth!" (Psalm 119:103, NRSV), and in Song of Solomon, "Your lips distill nectar, my bride; honey and milk are under your tongue" (Song of Solomon 4:11a, NRSV). In mystical eucharistic experience, the people become the Bride of Christ.

Wine, like the other elements, is found everywhere and brings joy and celebration. The story of Jesus turning water into wine symbolized the life of transformation available to us. We are the vessels. The ordinary water of our being can become the wine of joy when we are transformed from the inside out.

When we take these substances of bread and three cups into ourselves and let them do their work, we become what we eat. What these elements symbolize becomes us, is lived out in us, and helps bring our broken, separated parts back together to be healed.

In most celebrations of the Eucharist today, only bread and wine are used, but a priest will customarily add some water to the cup of wine. The water and wine cups were conflated into one cup. The cup of milk and honey, the most feminine of them all, was dropped, along with some of the other feminine imagery and yin energy.

I think it is time to restore the three cups to the Eucharistic celebrations by reclaiming the missing cup of water and the missing cup of milk and honey. Using all three cups would not be an innovation, but rather a restoration of early practice and might very well deepen our experience.

Here are excerpts from a eucharistic prayer found in *The Acts of John*:

And he asked for bread and gave thanks with these words: "What praise or what offering or what thanksgiving shall we name as we break this bread, but thee alone, Jesu? We glorify thy name of Father which was spoken by thee; we glorify thy name of Son which was spoken by thee. We glorify thine entering of the door; we glorify thy Resurrection that is shown us through thee."

(Acts of John 109[4])

The prayer continues by recalling some of the stories that Jesus tells. Each story is familiar to the people, so a single word brings the entire story to consciousness. "We glorify thy Seed, the Word, Grace, Faith, the Salt, the inexpressible Pearl, the Treasure, the Plough, the Net, the Greatness, the Diadem" (Acts of John 109).

This beautiful eucharistic prayer focuses on a theme rarely found in eucharistic prayers: the central teaching of Jesus regarding the Son of Man.

"We glorify him that for our sakes was called the Son of Man, the truth, repose, knowledge, power, commandment, confidence, hope, love, liberty, and refuge in thee. For thou alone, O Lord, are the Root of immortality and the fount of incorruption and the seat of the ages, who art called all these things on our account, that calling on thee through them we may know thy greatness, which at the present is invisible to us, but visible only to the pure as it is portrayed in your humanity only."

(Acts of John 109)

After offering this prayer, the liturgist takes the bread, which can be leavened now because people are relaxed. Who is in a hurry? Christ is Bread. The Bread is rising. The energy of the Spirit-filled community is rising. As people celebrate eucharistically, they experience what it feels like to be members of the same living Body.

If you were part of this primitive celebration, you would receive the bread and hear words like these: "May there be for me also a part with you," and "Peace be with you, my beloved" (Acts of John 109).

A Deep Sense of Knowing and Union

My hope is that in providing you with selections from eucharistic prayers you will get a sense of the variety of ways in which members of Christ's Risen Body celebrated together. The prayers are quite different and reflect a great diversity. I have already included selections from *The Didache, Apostolic Tradition of Hippolytus,* and *The Acts of John.*

Now I add two more, starting with the deeply mysterious *Gospel of Philip.* In the community where this Gospel originated, people assemble and move together into the Mystery following an identifiable sequence: "The Lord did everything in a mystery: a baptism, an anointing, a eucharist, a redemption, and a bridal chamber" (Gospel of Philip, NHL). Worship culminates in that deep sense of knowing and union identified as the bridal chamber. In later times these parts of the one sequence are separated into sacraments of baptism, confirmation, anointing for healing, eucharist, reconciliation, and marriage.

> Christ came to repair the separation which was from the beginning and again unite the two, and to give life to those who died as a result of the separation and unite them. But the woman is united to her husband in the bridal chamber. Indeed those who have been united in the bridal chamber will no longer be separated.
>
> (Gospel of Philip 70:13–17, NHL)

We have no actual text for this eucharistic liturgy and no clear description of what may have occurred "in the bridal chamber." Were the liturgies entirely extemporaneous, with leaders assisting the people in moving through the sequence as they became ready? Might there have been written liturgies that have been lost?

Even though we do not know the answer to these questions, we do have some teachings about the experience. The bridal chamber is a symbol of an even greater Mystery: the union of the soul with God. The concluding words of the *Authoritative Teaching* make this clear:

> The rational soul who wearied herself in seeking—she learned about God. She labored with inquiring, enduring distress in the body, wearing out her feet after the evangelists, learning about the Inscrutable One. She found her rising. She came to rest in him who is at rest. She reclined in the bridechamber. She ate of the banquet for which she had hungered. She partook of the immortal food. She found what she had sought after. She received rest from her labors, while the light that

shines forth upon her does not sink. To it belongs the glory and the power and the revelation for ever and ever. Amen.

(Authoritative Teaching 35:1–21, NHL).

Further, the community as a whole is called to become the Bride of Christ. Liturgical celebrations are designed to allow that reality to be embodied and experienced. Taking the time needed, the assembly of God moves deeper and deeper into the Mystery until all become one. Words become superfluous as the community of people move beyond words into the deep silence and rest.

19

Experiencing Resurrection
Through Baptism

As the family, friends, and followers of Jesus begin experiencing the Resurrected Jesus in themselves and one another, the Body of Christ becomes a living reality. How will new members be added to this Body? How will they enter into their own experience of resurrection?

From the early writings, it becomes clear that the communities of the Resurrected Jesus shared both their oral and written traditions and then offered baptism to those who were prepared and ready for the experience.

Before looking at some of the early baptismal practices, I think it would be useful to focus attention on Jesus' own experience of baptism.[1]

The Baptism of Jesus as Basic Pattern

All three of the Synoptic Gospels have the story of Jesus' baptism. Mark's Gospel begins with the ministry of John the Baptizer and the baptism of Jesus.

After being baptized, Jesus begins his ministry: "Jesus was about thirty years old when he began his work" (Luke 3:23, NRSV). What might he have been doing for the first thirty years of his life?

Jesus was a Jew growing up in a household whose members took their faith seriously. It would be accurate to assume that Jesus and his family followed the teachings and practices of first-century Judaism, including the sacrifice of animals in the Temple in Jerusalem. The Gospels of Matthew, Luke, and James provide the virgin birth stories, which are symbolic and mythic in character.[2] *The Infancy Gospel of Thomas,* not to be confused with *The Gospel of Thomas,* provides mythic and legendary stories about Jesus' childhood. The Gospel of Luke has a little story about Jesus at the age of twelve "sitting among the teachers, listening to them, and asking them questions. Everyone listening to him was astounded at his understanding and his responses" (Luke 4:46–47, SV).

Jesus is called the carpenter in Mark 6:3, and he is called the son of the carpenter in Matthew 13:55. Which might he have been? Or might both be the case: Jesus becoming a carpenter, following his father's trade?

What might his personal life have been like? Who were his friends and associates? What were his interests? How did he spend his time? Did he do any traveling? Besides his native Judaism, what philosophies and religious teachings might he have explored or studied? What might have been going on in Jesus' life as he celebrated his thirtieth birthday?

Essentially, we have very little information about the historic Jesus prior to his baptism. Mark describes the setting as follows:

So, John the Baptizer appeared in the wilderness calling for baptism and a change of heart that leads to forgiveness of sins. And everyone from the Judean countryside and all the residents of Jerusalem streamed out to him and got baptized by him in the Jordan river, admitting their sins. And John wore a mantel made of camel hair and had a leather belt around his waist and lived on locusts and raw honey.
(Mark 1:4–6, SV).

Picture this hairy prophet preaching out in the wilderness alongside the Jordan River with large crowds coming out to hear him. One of the people in the crowd is Jesus. What might have brought Jesus out to hear John? Is he there out of curiosity to see for himself what is going on? Might there be some part of Jesus that is searching? Are there other motivations that flash into your mind?

Whatever it is that impels Jesus to come out to the Jordan, visualize him at the river listening to this hairy prophet shouting in the wilderness. What does John have to say? Listen now to his message as recorded in the *The Lost Gospel Q*: "Brood of vipers, who warned you to flee from the impending doom?" When his opening salvo is calling people a bunch of snakes, why would anyone want to stick around for the rest? Or is this John's brash way of getting people's attention? Those who are not chased off by his opening words hear John's challenge: "Produce good fruit. Prove that your hearts are really changed" (The Lost Gospel 2, Borg-Powelson-Riegert Version; see For Further Reading and Study).

So what does John really mean by this? What sort of change of heart is he talking about? How might Jesus be responding to this message to change his heart?

Before anyone can fully grasp what John means, he lands another punch: "Do not think of saying to yourselves, 'We are Abraham's children' because, I tell you, God can produce children for Abraham right out of these rocks."

Family ancestry normally defines identity for first-century people much more strongly than today, so we may not fully understand the impact of these words. Part of the power in John's message is that in one stroke he wipes out reliance on family roots. Is he putting anything else in its place?

One more blow follows. This time John has a verbal axe in his hand: "Even now the axe is aimed at the roots of the tree, so that any tree that fails to produce good fruit will be cut down and thrown on the fire."

Hearing words like this, how might the listeners respond? And what might be going on in the mind and heart of Jesus? According to the story, one of the listeners' questions is this, "So what shall we do?"

John responds with very practical things people can do: "Whoever has two shirts must share with someone who has none. Whoever has food should do the same."

Even tax collectors come to be baptized; they ask John, "Teacher, what shall we do?" John answers them, "Charge no more than the official rate."

Soldiers also ask him, "And what about us?" John replies, "Don't harass people. No more extortion. Be satisfied with your pay."

Assuming that Jesus is neither a tax collector nor a soldier but possibly a carpenter, what in John's message might be speaking directly to Jesus? What sort of change of heart and change in behavior might Jesus be feeling he needed to make?

Jesus responds to John's message and moves forward in the crowd to be baptized.

The story of Jesus' baptism is succinct, yet it provides the essentials for our understanding when we approach it with at least three questions: What is happening in Jesus? How does his experience provide the paradigm for baptism of others in the first-century Jesus movement? And what are the implications for us now?

As many times as I have studied the baptism of Jesus, I still do not fully grasp this Mystery. I feel some fear and wonder. Even so, I approach this story of Jesus' baptism and invite you to dive into it with me. With questions seeking to understand, with our mental faculties fully working, and with hearts opening as fully as possible, let's plunge in. Here is the story:

> In those days Jesus came from Nazareth of Galilee and was baptized by John in the Jordan. And just as he was coming up out of the water, he saw the heavens torn apart and the Spirit descending like a dove on him. And a voice came from heaven, "You are my Son, the Beloved; with you I am well pleased."
> (Mark 1:9–11, NRSV).

Picture the scene: it is the Jordan River. Quite literally, what do rivers do? The fact that they move, carrying water from one place to another, is significant. Water itself is a symbol of the unconscious. To be baptized means to be immersed in water. The process involves going down and then coming up, which may seem obvious but is very important symbolically and suggests that one begins by moving down into the depths of the unconscious.

Imagine, if you will, the various ways of getting into water: one can enter gently, little by little. One can jump in, dive in, and so on. Likewise, one can enter with a wide variety of feelings—everything from temerity to exuberance. The same is true when entering the waters of the unconscious.

The deeper one goes, the darker it gets and the more pressure one feels. The same is true when entering the depths of the unconscious. With this in mind, we might ask what Jesus may have found in the depths of his own soul?

There may have been much more occurring for Jesus than is recorded in the story, but this part is clear: coming out of the water, Jesus hears a voice, saying, "You are my beloved Son."

Where does this voice originate? In the later Gospel of Matthew, the voice says, "This is my beloved Son." It appears to be addressed to the people around. But in Mark's earlier version, the voice is speaking directly to Jesus and may very well be an inner voice Jesus is hearing. He knows he is accepted and loved. What might it feel like to be totally loved?

The voice also says, "I am pleased with you." If this is the voice of God within, what would it be like for Jesus to know that he is giving God pleasure? The depth of the relationship is clear. Jesus feels connected to the universe in a personal way as he cries out, "Abba!" which is a childlike expression similar in English to saying "Daddy!" or "Mama!"

The heavens open; some versions say the heavens are "torn apart." We can begin imagining what sort of breakthrough this may be for Jesus!

Then comes the Spirit, "like a dove." In the story of Noah and the Flood, toward the end of the voyage, Noah opens a window and a dove comes. The symbol of the dove suggests peace and gentleness.

Notice the opposites here; a tearing open is followed by peace. How true that is in our human experience! After a stormy disruption comes a calm. Something dies, and something new comes alive. Baptism for Jesus is an experience of dying and rising again. In his baptism is his resurrection.

Some versions of the baptism story say, "You are my beloved son; today I have begotten you." In the deepest sense, Jesus is being born anew.

Today the phrase "being born again" has great meaning for some people; for others, it suggests an orientation with very negative connotations. If we can move past any present associations, then we may see Jesus and his experience fresh and unclouded.

A line from The Gospel of Philip may help: "As soon as Christ went down into the water, he came out laughing . . ." (Gospel of Philip 74:29 NHL). This part of the story is rooted in Psalm 2, which says, "You are my son; today I have begotten you" and also, "He who sits in the heavens laughs" (Psalm 2:7,

4, NRSV). By implication, we see that Jesus and his Father are laughing together! Can you recall very happy times when you and your parent or you and your child have been joyously laughing together? When children and parents are enjoying each other, this is just a taste of what cosmic joy is all about when someone is born anew. After an experience like this, how might Jesus' relationship with God be described?

Immediately following his baptism, Jesus goes into the wilderness to sort out what has happened and discover how he will live in this new relationship. What is expected of him? What will he choose to do next? What other questions might now be in his mind and heart?

Baptism into the Risen Body

With the baptism of Jesus clearly in mind, we now consider how baptism is experienced by those who are becoming members of the Risen Body of Christ.

The most complete description is provided for us in *The Apostolic Tradition* written by Hippolytus, a bishop in Rome, ca. 217 C.E. Hippolytus reveals a much earlier tradition originating in the second, possibly even the first century.

In order to get the feeling and spiritual force of what it would have been like to become a member of a community of the Resurrected Jesus in the earliest days of the church, I invite you to imagine yourself as a person seeking baptism in the time of Hippolytus.

According to *The Apostolic Tradition*, you would have participated with others in a long period of instruction and preparation. One of the Gospels might have served as the basic course of study. The process of baptism itself begins on Thursday, when you are instructed to take a bath, wash yourself thoroughly, and pray that you may become free of all outer and inner impurities. On Friday you fast all day. On Saturday you and all the others being baptized are gathered together by the bishop. Each person kneels in prayer before the bishop. You feel the bishop's hand upon your head as he prays that all evil spirits may leave you and never return. Then the bishop breathes into your face and anoints you with oil on your forehead, ears, and nose. Then he raises you up to stand. You spend all Saturday night in vigil, listening to reading and instruction.

On Sunday morning you bring your offering for the Eucharist, which might be the bread, water, milk and honey, or wine. You and all the others gather at a stream or wherever there is moving water. Very early in the morning as dawn is breaking you hear the first cock crow, and everyone knows it is time to begin. The bishop gives thanks over the water.

All who are to be baptized remove their clothing and jewelry. Long hair must not be tied back but allowed to fall freely. As you stand there, naked as the day you were born, you remember the words of Jesus: "When you strip without being ashamed, and you take your clothes and put them under your feet like little children and trample them, then you will see the son of the living one and you will not be afraid" (Gospel of Thomas 37, SV).

First the little ones are baptized. If they can speak for themselves, they do so; if not, their parents or other relatives speak for them. Then the adults are baptized.

A priest asks you if you renounce Satan and all his works. As you respond to this question, the priest anoints you with olive oil and you hear him saying, "Let all spirits depart from thee."

You go down into the water with a deacon and stand there waist high. You hear the first question: "Do you believe in God, the Father Almighty?" You respond with your faith and trust, saying, "I believe." A priest takes your right hand and turns you to make sure you are facing east, symbol of the rising sun and the resurrection. The priest places a hand on your forehead, immerses you backwards into the water, and raises you up.

You hear a second question: "Do you believe in Christ Jesus, the Son of God, who was born of the Holy Spirit of the Virgin Mary, and was crucified under Pontius Pilate, and was dead and buried, and rose again on the third day, alive from the dead, and ascended into heaven, and sat at the right hand of the Father, and will come to judge the living and the dead?" You respond with your faith and trust, saying, "I believe." And you are immersed in the water a second time.

You hear a third question: "Do you believe in the Holy Spirit, and the holy church, and the resurrection of the flesh?" You respond with your faith and trust, saying, "I believe." And you are immersed in the water a third time.

As you come out of the water a priest anoints you with oil again and says, "I anoint you with holy oil in the name of Jesus Christ." This is the oil of thanksgiving. Now it is time to dry yourself off and put on your new white clothing symbolizing your being clothed with Christ. It is time to walk from the stream and enter the church. You are now a living member of Christ's Risen Body. You have risen in the flesh.

Everyone rejoices with you, and the bishop gives thanks again with one more laying on of hands and one more anointing on your forehead, saying, "I anoint you with oil in the Lord, the Father Almighty and Christ Jesus and the Holy Spirit."

You might also hear the bishop praying spontaneously:

Glory be to You, hidden power that is united with us in baptism!
Glory be to You, ineffable power that is in baptism!
Glory be to You, renewal through which are renewed the baptized who take hold of you with affection!

(Acts of Thomas 132–33[3])

Signing each person on the forehead the bishop says, "The Lord be with you," and each one responds, "And with your spirit."

Immediately everyone joins in heartfelt prayer for all who have just been baptized. The prayer might be expressed this way:

> Be their Guide in a land of error;
> Be their Physician in a land of sickness;
> Be their Rest in a land of the weary;
> Sanctify them in a land polluted;
> Be the Physician of their bodies and souls;
> Make them Your Holy Temples,
>   and let Your Holy Spirit dwell in them!
>
>   (Acts of Thomas 120–21).

At the close of prayer everyone shares the kiss of peace. Then follows the Eucharist of Bread and Three Cups.

Resurrection Is Now or Never

The Gospel of Philip is clear in making connections between the baptism of Jesus and baptism for everyone else: "Jesus revealed himself at the Jordan: it was the fullness of the kingdom of heaven. He who was begotten before everything was begotten anew. He who was once anointed was anointed anew. He who was redeemed in turn redeemed others" (Gospel of Philip 70:34–71:5, NHL). The primordial pattern is in the experience of Jesus. Can we enter into the same experience? If so, what is involved?

Philip explains further: "Those who say that the Lord died first and then rose up are in error, for he rose up and then died" (Gospel of Philip 56:16–17, NHL).

What might have died for Jesus in his baptism? And what rose up in him? What came alive? A few years later Jesus dies on a cross, but his essential death, burial, and resurrection came during his baptism. After that experience Jesus began living the resurrected life. This is the essential pattern for his followers.

Just in case this isn't clear, *The Gospel of Philip* goes on to say that "those who say they will die first and then rise are in error. If they do not first receive the resurrection while they live, when they die they will receive nothing" (Gospel of Philip 73:1–3, NHL).

If you thought you would die and then go to heaven, you may be in for a big disappointment. Baptism symbolizes the inner death and resurrection that is needed if you and I are to live fully right now. Resurrection is now or never!

The Gospel of Philip continues, So also when speaking about baptism they say, "baptism is a great thing," because if they receive it they will live. . . . Some are afraid lest they rise naked. Because of this they wish to rise in the flesh, and they do not know it is those who wear the flesh who are naked. . . . It is those who unclothe themselves who are not naked. . . . It is necessary that we put on the living man. Therefore, when he is about to go down into the water, he unclothes himself, in order that he may put on the living man.

> (Gospel of Philip 73:5–8, 56:27–31, 75:22–24, NHL)

Here is a clear connection with the teachings of Jesus about the Son of Man becoming an authentic human being. When baptism is effective, the seed of our true humanity bursts open, and new life begins to grow within us.

The potential of baptism is expressed in *The Acts of Thomas* this way: "This baptism is forgiveness of sins. It brings to new birth a light that is shed around. It brings to new birth the new human being, renews the thoughts, mingles soul and body, raises up the new human being in three-fold manner, and is partaker in forgiveness of sins" (Acts of Thomas 131).

Experience and Ritual

What might be the relationship between the ritual of baptism and the experience it symbolizes?

If one goes down into the water and comes up without having received anything and says, 'I am a Christian,' he has borrowed the name at interest. But if he receives the Holy Spirit, he has the name as a gift. He who has received a gift does not have to give it back, but of him who has borrowed it at interest, payment is demanded. This is the way it happens to one when one experiences a mystery.

> (Gospel of Philip 64:23–31, NHL)

Baptism, like any ritual, can be hollow and meaningless. When little is expected, little happens. It is robbed of its life. When that occurs, why bother?

On the other hand, suppose we were to take the baptism of Jesus as our model and embrace, unafraid and with full faith, the early practice of the communities of the Resurrected Jesus. We might enter deeply into the experience of Jesus. Our relationship with the Source of Life might come more fully alive. The seed of our true humanity might burst open, sprout, and begin to grow from within us. Then when anyone asks, "Is resurrection real to you?" we might respond with rich, full, joyous laughter.

20

Time Out
in the Wilderness

All the evidence points toward something very powerful and life changing occurring in Jesus during his baptism, something so powerful that the very next thing he needed to do was to take some time out, alone. Mark's Gospel describes the scenario this way: "And the Spirit immediately drove him out into the wilderness" (Mark 1:12, NRSV).

As with all symbols in Holy Scripture, the outer, literal place is set before us as a way of describing an inner experience. Jesus leaves the familiar and enters a nearby wilderness so that he can simultaneously enter into the natural, wild, untamed, free places within himself.

Mark says that the Spirit "drives" him there. Luke and Matthew say that the Spirit "leads" him there. In your own experiences, have there been times when you have felt very driven? Do you recall other times when you have felt gently led by the Spirit? The question remains open: was Jesus led or driven, or might he have felt aspects of both?

"He was in the wilderness forty days, tempted by Satan" (Mark 1:13, NRSV). Consider the symbolism of forty days. The Flood lasts forty days and forty nights. The Israelites are in the wilderness forty years. Moses spends forty days on the top of Mount Sinai receiving the Ten Commandments. Scouts check out the promised land for forty days. David is thirty when he becomes king and then rules for forty years. The number forty is a recurring symbol in the stories, one that is rooted in the time required for something new to be born; it usually takes about forty weeks to make a baby from the love making to the birthing. So whenever we see the symbol of forty, we know it means "enough time."

Jesus spends forty days in the wilderness—in other words, enough time to do what is needed. When he goes into the wilderness within himself, who does he encounter there? Satan.

Questions from the Instructor

Recall the Garden of Eden story where Satan comes in the form of a serpent.

With that story in mind, consider the Creation Story from the perspective of *The Hypostasis of the Archons* and *On the Origin of the World*, two third-century documents found in the Nag Hammadi Library. These interpretations may be different from ones you have heard before; they may even be startling.

In these texts, the serpent is "the Female Spiritual Principle, the Instructor." She teaches them, saying:

> "What did he say to you? Was it, 'From every tree in the Garden shall you eat; yet—from the tree of recognizing evil and good do not eat?'"
>
> The carnal Woman said, "Not only did he say 'Do not eat,' but even 'Do not touch it; for the day you eat from it, with death you are going to die.'"
>
> And the snake, the Instructor, said, "With death you shall not die; for it was out of jealousy that he said this to you. Rather your eyes shall open and you shall become like gods, recognizing evil and good." And the Female Instructing Principle was taken away from the Snake, and she left it behind merely a thing of the earth.
>
> (Hypostasis of the Archons 89:31–90:13, NHL)

> Now Eve believed the words of the instructor. She looked at the tree. And she saw that it was beautiful and magnificent, and she desired it. She took some of its fruit and ate, and she gave to her husband also, and he ate too. Then their mind opened. For when they ate, the light of knowledge shone for them. When they put on shame, they knew that they were naked with regard to knowledge.
>
> (On the Origin of the World 119:7–15, NHL)

By engaging in dialogue with the serpent, the eyes of Adam and Eve are in fact opened. They are beginning to come to consciousness. Tasting of the fruit is a necessary part of the process. They recognize that they are lacking in knowledge and are now open to learning.

Over the ages, the serpent has received some very bad press. Yet Satan actually has a very significant function as the Instructor who is raising questions, getting people to think, and helping to bring people to consciousness. So who is this Satan with Jesus in the wilderness? Might she be the same female spiritual principle who comes in the form of a serpent to be his instructor?

Mark tells us that Jesus spends forty days encountering the serpent inside himself. Matthew and Luke provide us with some of the dialogue between them: "If you are the Son of God, command these stones to become loaves of bread" (Matthew 4:3, NRSV).

In his baptism experience, Jesus feels that he is a beloved son and now that relationship is challenged with "If you are the Son of God. . . ." Shortly after making the breakthrough into a new awareness, Jesus is confronted with doubts and challenges. Movement forward is followed by a pull backward.

Jesus responds to the first temptation, saying, "One does not live by bread alone, but by every word that comes from the mouth of God" (Matt. 4:4, NRSV). Jesus is quoting a line from Deuteronomy 8:3. What might it mean to live by every word that comes from the mouth of God? In the Creation story, the Word speaks and things come into being. The Word fully expressed releases creativity.

In a second challenge to Jesus' relationship with God, Satan took Jesus "to the holy city and placed him on the pinnacle of the temple, saying to him, 'If you are the Son of God, throw yourself down; for it is written, "He will command his angels concerning you" and "On their hands they will bear you up, so that you will not dash your foot against a stone."'" (Matt. 4:5–6, NRSV).

In other words, "You can do anything now and God will protect you! Jump off the top of the Temple and the angels will catch you!" There seems to be an inflated feeling, "Now I can do anything, even foolish things, and I will be protected." The exhilaration of a spiritual breakthrough can go to one's head. Inflation can also do damage to the newly discovered relationship.

Jesus considers what Satan has proposed and then responds, "Again it is written, 'Do not put the Lord your God to the test!'" (Matt. 4:7, NRSV). Perhaps this experience led Jesus later to offer the "Lord's Prayer" with the phrase "Lead us not into temptation," now translated by liturgical scholars as "Save us from the time of trial."

In a very real sense, the Instructor is playing "Devil's Advocate," throwing down challenges that bring out Jesus' creativity. An adversary can serve a very important function as challenges bring spiritual growth.

Satan has one more suggestion. Taking Jesus to a very high mountain, Satan shows him all the kingdoms of the world and their splendor and says to him, "All these I will give you, if you will fall down and worship me." Jesus replies, "Away with you, Satan! for it is written, 'Worship the Lord your God, and serve only him'" (Matt. 4:10, NRSV). Jesus is offered opportunities to misuse the new power he received in his baptism. Among them is the temptation to take authority and rule over all the kingdoms of the world. Jesus says "No" to this misuse of power. By facing this temptation squarely, Jesus is able to bring it to consciousness, consider it, and put it aside.

With Jesus and the inner Instructor are also the "wild beasts." In a literal outer wilderness, there may be many wild animals. As symbolic figures in the wilderness story, what might the wild beasts represent within Jesus? Might they be his wild, untamed, natural energies? Might they include his desires, his sexuality, and all his native powers?

Jesus has a wide range of choices regarding what to do with his wild beasts. He can avoid them, chase them away, kill them, give them free reign, even embrace them. In the story, Jesus is simply with the wild beasts. Jesus is comfortable with his wild, natural energies. There is no need to ignore, deny, suppress, or destroy them as some forms of religion teach. Nor does he allow them to run rampant and dissipate his energy. He is with them and in relationship with them.

Jesus is "with the wild beasts and the angels minister to him" (Mark 1:13, RSV). There is an old tradition of people being visited by angels as Sarah and Abraham are by the three men who come to them and share meals and hospitality with them in their tent (Gen. 18:1–15). From this comes the phrase "Do not neglect to show hospitality to strangers, for by doing that some have entertained angels without knowing it" (Heb. 13:2, NRSV). Angels are messengers from God with something to say to us. Another person may function as an angel. In the wilderness experience, Jesus is by himself, indicating that these angels are within him serving as messengers.

Having been driven or led into the wilderness by the Spirit, Jesus remains there for forty days in dialogue with Satan, the Instructor, his wild beasts, and his angels. "Jesus fasted forty days and forty nights, and afterward he was hungry" (Matt. 4:2, RSV). Well, who wouldn't be hungry after fasting forty days? At the deeper level, what is Jesus actually hungering for? Later in his teachings Jesus says to us, "Blessed are those who hunger and thirst for righteousness, for they will be filled" (Matt. 5:6, NRSV). Might he be speaking from his own experience?

Jesus tells the Instructor that one lives by the Word of God. According to the Gospels, Jesus keeps listening to the Word of God in prayer, which for him is dialogue: speaking, listening, and asking questions.

Feeling the Anointing of the Spirit

As Jesus leaves the wilderness, the Spirit goes with him. In his first recorded sermon, Jesus proclaims, "The Spirit of the Lord is upon me, because he has anointed me" (Luke 4:18a, NRSV). Jesus feels the anointing of the Spirit, which serves for several specific purposes.

"He has anointed me to bring good news to the poor" (Luke 4:18, NRSV). Might Jesus have known what it is to be poor and experience good news? When did he become aware of his call to preaching? Was it as he was listening to John and during his wilderness time?

Later in the Gospels we are given two versions of the Beatitudes from Jesus: "Blessed are you who are poor, for yours is the kingdom of God" (Luke 6:20, NRSV); "Blessed are the poor *in spirit*, for theirs is the kingdom of heaven" (Matt. 5:3, NRSV). Whom do you think Jesus is addressing in his message—the poor or the poor in spirit or both?

"He has sent me to proclaim release to the captives" (Luke 4:18, NRSV). To whom is he addressing release—those who are captive to outer powers like the Romans or those held captive by inner powers? Assuming that Jesus speaks from experience, how might he have known his own release from captivity?

"And recovering of sight to the blind" (Luke 4:18, RSV). Adam and Eve have their eyes opened through their dialogue with the serpent, the Instructor. Might the same serpent have opened the eyes of Jesus to new ways of seeing? If so, Jesus knows firsthand what it is for one who is blind to recover sight.

"To set at liberty those who are oppressed" (Luke 4:18, RSV). Follow Jesus through the rest of his life and one of the outstanding characteristics is his freedom to be himself, to live and proclaim the reality he knows regardless of the consequences. He has found the seed of his true humanity; it has burst open, is sprouting and growing. As a result, Jesus is content to proclaim the message and then leave it with those "who have eyes to see" and "ears to hear."

"And to proclaim the year of the Lord's amnesty" (Luke 4:18, SV). Amnesty includes both pardon and forgiveness of all past offenses. How might Jesus have experienced his amnesty? We do not know what his life was like during his first thirty years, but amnesty for thirty years of behaviors might be quite a release. Now Jesus is proclaiming to all who will hear that this is the year of the Lord's amnesty for them as well.

And how might the people be responding to this message? Luke says that "all spoke well of him and were amazed at the gracious words that came from his mouth. They said, 'Is not this Joseph's son?'" (Luke 4:22, NRSV). On the one hand the response is spontaneously very welcoming, "How wonderful!" The other side of resistance comes quickly with a challenge, "Who is this Jesus? We know him and his family." A parallel passage has the people asking, "Can anything good come out of Nazareth?" (John 1:46, NRSV). Immediately following his first sermon is this attempt to discredit Jesus because of his town of origin.

Dialogues and challenges continue for the rest of Jesus' life. All the way to the end, Jesus lives the Spirit-filled life.

If You Will Not Know Yourself, You Dwell in Poverty

Continuing to explore the continuities between Jesus' experience and teachings with the experience of members of Christ's Risen Body, I draw your attention to one of Jesus' teachings recorded in *The Gospel of Thomas*: "The Kingdom is inside of you, and it is outside of you. When you come to know yourselves, then you will become known, and you will realize that it is you who are the sons of the living Father. But if you will not know yourselves, you dwell in poverty and it is you who are that poverty" (Gospel of Thomas 3, NHL).

The necessity of discovering what is within us is made even more startlingly clear in this saying from Jesus. "That which you have will save you if you bring it forth from yourselves. That which you do not have within you will kill you if you do not have it within you" (Gospel of Thomas 70, NHL).

This teaching is echoed later in *The Teachings of Silvanus*: "For no one who wants to will be able to know God as he actually is, nor Christ, nor the Spirit, nor the chorus of angels, nor even the archangels, and the thrones of the spirits, and the exalted lordships, and the Great Mind. If you do not know yourself, you will not be able to know all of these" (Teachings of Silvanus 116:28—117:5, NHL).

Two more powerful one-liners follow that you might want to copy and put on a card where you can view them: "Open the door for yourself that you may know what is; Knock on yourself that the Word may open for you" (Teachings of Silvanus 117:6–7, NHL).

Our lifelong journey involves calling on the Spirit to guide us in exploring the depths of ourselves as we interact with the outer world.

I Sing from My Heart to You

This song from *The Sybilline Oracles*[1] about Jesus' baptism reveals how he gives expression to the Spirit-filled life.

> I sing from my heart to You, Eternal Christ,
>   to whom the Most High gives Life and rebirth.
> You were raised up the second time according to the flesh,
>   when you were washed in the streams of the river Jordan.
> You move with gleaming foot
>   sweeping the waves.
> You escape the fire, and you are the first to see delightful God
>   coming in the spirit on the white wings of a dove.
> A pure flower blooms,
>   fountains burst forth.
> You show the Way to people
>   and point us to heavenly paths.
> You teach all with wise words
>   and come to encounter and persuade the unenlightened ones.
> You walk the waves;
>   you heal the sickness of people.
> You raise the dead
>   and repel many woes.

From one wallet You give abundance of bread
    when the house of David brings forth a shoot.
Your hands hold the whole world
    the earth and heaven and sea.
You flash like lightning on the earth
    as the two begotten from each other's sides[2] once saw You when
You first shone forth. It all comes to pass
    when earth rejoices in the hope of a child
        (Sibylline Oracles, Book 6, lines 1–20, John Butcher version).

21

Endings, Transitions, New Beginnings, Fresh Perspective

The biggest and most unfathomable Mystery is the gift of life itself. There really is no logical reason for anything at all to exist, yet here it is—an array of billions of galaxies including our own local galaxy, complete with the solar system, our own beautiful blue planet Earth, and our lives. It is extraordinary but true; we are each given a bit of life and of consciousness for brief moments in eternal time. We are infinitesimally tiny specks, hardly worth mentioning. Yet we are part of this most amazing incomprehensible system.

Once upon a time there was nothing at all: no sound, no light, no stuff, and of course no human beings. Then about fifteen billion years ago, give or take a few years, there was a Big Bang: out of Silence came Sound, out of Darkness came Light, out of No Thing began forming Every Thing, out of Unconscious began emerging Consciousness!

As we begin pondering the Mystery of life in general and our own lives in particular, then how can we help but realize that the natural state of human beings is ecstatic wonder?

Within this wondrous mysterious life are identifiable repeating cycles, and one of the most important of these is the fourfold process of death, entombment, resurrection, and ascension. These four illustrate the paschal process that is, in fact, lived out repeatedly in our lives as endings, transitions, new beginnings, and fresh perspectives.

My intention in this chapter is to review these four and invite you to consider where you are in the paschal process.

Within our life, we experience death, symbolized by Good Friday. We experience endings that take many forms—not just literal death, but all the little deaths that we go through as human beings.

There is the death of a loved one—a person or an animal. Children sometimes become first acquainted with death when a favorite pet dies. The death of a dog or a cat or a guinea pig or a bird can be a real shock for a child. Children sometimes experience the death of a parent, but these days it is more likely that they first experience the divorce of their parents; that, too, can be a "little death" for a child.

Adults experience little deaths through the death of another, through separation, through divorce, through termination at work, through company downsizings that leave them out in the cold. Little deaths include the death of cherished ideas or the shattering of plans, hopes, and dreams. Little deaths include rejection letters received from college or graduate school applications. Another is the realization that the project you have been working on isn't going to materialize. A little death may occur any time you realize that something you cared about is over. No doubt you can illustrate from your own life and from the lives of others some additional examples of little deaths. Our wondrous life is filled with them.

Just as it can be difficult to face the reality of death and accept our own mortality, so it can be very painful to face the reality of a little death. But no matter how much we try to deny it or explain it away or pretend it isn't happening, the reality persists.

With that reality comes a host of feelings, including anger at the person or people we think have caused it, anger at ourselves for not doing something we might have done to prevent it, anger at the situation, and sometimes anger at God. Isn't God supposed to be in charge? So why is this happening? And why is this happening to me?

Sooner or later we need to accept what has happened; it is over. The ending has come to the job, the relationship, the idea, the hope, the dream, whatever it might be.

Next comes Holy Saturday, the entombment, the time of transition. Others may try to cheer us up and tell us it is all going to get better. While we are in our transition time filled with confusion, anxiety, and a host of other feelings, it is sometimes difficult to be hopeful about the future.

It is rather like trying to tell a caterpillar inside his cocoon that he is going to be a butterfly one of these days. Our transition time can be just as much of a metamorphosis as it is for that caterpillar.

In our more cynical moments, we may even find ourselves feeling like the caterpillar whose attention had been drawn to a butterfly flying freely overhead. The caterpillar says, "You'll never get me up in one of those things!"

The bad news is that you still have to go through this transition time. The good news is that the Resurrected Jesus goes through this with you, just as Jesus went through his own painful death and entombment before the surprise of resurrection.

And resurrection is a surprise; it often occurs when you least expect it. One day you wake up and the sun is, in fact, shining. You realize that it is a new day, you have survived the change, and you now have a new life opening up in ways you might never have dreamed.

Resurrection is the new life. It is a new relationship with someone where there had been a serious break before. It is a new relationship with another person. It is recognizing that you yourself have changed; you have become a new person in Christ. In some way or other we discover that we are maturing in Christ, in spite of ourselves.

Everyone wants the resurrection experience, which is why Easter is more popular than Good Friday. Most of us would prefer to experience our resurrection as soon as possible. Who really wants the pain, grief, and anxiety of transition times? We would much prefer an easier way. Some forms of religion stress only the positive side of life and promise people what they want to hear. Sometimes an overly positive religion can do great damage because sooner or later the negative side of life appears, along with feelings of great disillusionment.

Never underestimate the importance of being disillusioned; having your illusions vanish may be very healthy. Can you thank God for your disillusions? Can you thank God, as one country western record puts it, for unanswered prayers? Our society is based on instant gratification. Any time we do not get what we want and do not get it right away, we may be tempted to feel angry and upset. But not getting what we want and learning a bit of patience can actually be quite healthy for us. It could even build our character.

Speaking of character, let's just forget the cult of personality, where appearances are the primary concern, and switch to character building, where we learn how to become genuine people with the inner strength of the Resurrected Jesus. In the closing verse of the Gospel of Matthew, the Resurrected Jesus says, "Remember, I am with you always, to the end of the age" (Matt. 28:20, NRSV).

New life will come. We are different, and the circumstances of our lives may be changed from the way they were before, from what we had expected, and from what we had been hoping. When the new life comes, we are experiencing a little resurrection, a new beginning.

There is a fourth part of the sequence, ascension. For years and years, ascension made little or no sense to me because I was taking it literally. I thought ascension meant the body of Jesus was shooting up into the heavens without any sort of spacecraft. The ascension had no experiential meaning for me. I even belonged to a group called the "Guild of the Ascension" and prayed daily this prayer: "Grant, we beseech thee, Almighty God, that like as we do believe thy only-begotten Son our Lord Jesus Christ to have ascended into the heavens, so we may also in heart and mind thither ascend, and with him continually dwell." I repeated that prayer hundreds of times but still didn't have the foggiest notion what it was all about, so I quit the Guild of the Ascension.

Later I came to realize my problem; I had not matured enough to experience ascension in my own life. Now ascension has deep meaning for me. In my own spiritual life, I have died, I have been in the tomb, I have risen from the dead, and I am experiencing ascension. I am beginning to understand.

Ascension is the fresh perspective that we are given after, and only after, we have gone through our endings, transitions, and new beginnings. Ascension is that higher place where we can review, which means "view again," usually from a higher spot, and look at the big picture. You simply cannot do that very well when you are hanging on the cross of one of your little deaths, or struggling inside the four walls of your transition tomb, or even when you are out of the tomb walking in a new light of day or trying out your wings like the former caterpillar turned butterfly. In the liturgical year, we normally celebrate resurrection for forty days before we mention ascension. The symbol of forty means "enough time" to accomplish what is needed.

Once we have taken the time needed to go through the first three stages, then we may come to an ascended place where we are able to say, "So that's what I have been through!"

Four parts of the process are in sequence: endings, transitions, new beginnings, fresh perspective. These are repeating cycles in our lives, if we are really living. Sometimes we do not remain in the ascended position very long before we are confronted with another little death and the cycle begins once more.

I would stress that these cycles go in sequence. There is a clear progression of spiritual experience: one awareness follows another. We learn a little at a time. You cannot skip lessons.

Those who have been through these spiritual cycles at least once know what the Great Paschal Mystery of the liturgical year is all about. You begin understanding these Mysteries as you actually experience them.

Knowing that these four are all part of a cyclical natural mysterious process can help us go through them and grow. The alternative, of course, is not to go through them but to do all we can to avoid them. Ironically, we may then discover that our soul has died, and the chances of its being resurrected become less and less likely. "Where there is life, there is hope," yet force of habit and resistance to change can keep a soul in solitary confinement from which there is no exit.

I have seen people whose souls appear to have died. Outwardly they seem healthy enough and are walking around, functioning, even holding down jobs and maintaining relationships of sorts. But the light seems to have gone out; there is no visible spark left. If someone in such a condition is unaware of what has happened, can there be any hope?

Fortunately, when one sees and feels his or her own inner deadness, then the process can begin and resurrection is possible. This matter is very serious, and I feel a warning is needed: the longer one remains with a dead soul inside, the more the odds are against new life rising.

Individuals go through these cycles, and so do groups of people and churches and institutions. Can you think of any situation that is not affected by these cycles of change? If you think you have found one, you have proba-bly discovered a monument to something that has already died. Monuments do not change. They just stand there and weather away until they collapse.

We have some choices: either to resist change and turn ourselves into stone monuments; or to embrace change, to keep close to the Risen Christ in prayer, and to move through our endings, transitions, new beginnings, and fresh per-spectives as gracefully as possible.

22

Rising in Our Dying

Even with the rapid advances in medical science and technology, the death rate remains the same—one death per person. The sooner each of us faces the inevitability of death, the greater the opportunity for living with intention and care.

Including Death in Our Plans

I recall when the current fear was that of "becoming a vegetable." The focus was on "quality of life" and when to "pull the plug." The Living Will became popular and was quickly followed by Medical Power of Attorney. You choose someone you trust to make the decisions around the complicated questions related to having no "extraordinary measures." Next came the Right to Die movement and a shift from "letting nature take its course" to being proactive in ending one's own life.

Nonprofit Health Maintenance Organizations were formed with primary attention given to staying healthy. Taking responsibility for one's own health makes a shift away from "leaving it all in the hands of the doctor." Alternative medicine modalities become popular. Will you choose Western medicine or Eastern medicine or a blend?

Now Managed Care positions the medical business to maximize profits. The fear of becoming a vegetable is being replaced with the fear of having one's life curtailed when it is no longer profitable. Why keep you alive when the costs of your medical care are eating up corporate profits? Discussion and debate on these and countless other issues are likely to be with us for a long time to come.

Meanwhile, I have gone ahead and made my plans. My grandfather lived to be one hundred years old and died a few months later. My father lived into his ninetieth year and died on St. John the Evangelist Day. Because I value both of their examples, I plan to combine them by living to be one hundred and dying on the following St. John's Day, December 27, 2036. I have put the date on my calendar!

For my death itself, I prefer that it not be a violent one. I would rather not die in an auto accident or in a fire or from being murdered or executed. My best friend died at the age of thirty-three under very violent circumstances. Even though his life was short, it continues to make enormous creative impact on my life and the lives of many millions of people two thousand years later. His way of living and dying still evokes the best in our human potential. His death has proved to be redemptive. So if it becomes necessary for me to die violently for something that matters, then I would hope I would accept it, even embrace it.

I would rather not die from cancer or any other painful or debilitating disease. Death by starvation is not my idea of a good time either. I have a history of asthma and have already experienced a respiratory arrest. I did not breathe on my own for two hours but was "hand bagged" by a skilled and very patient emergency room nurse. He could have given up after ten minutes or half an hour, or even an hour, but he kept going until my lungs finally resumed functioning on their own. Because I have "been there and done that," I do not want to die gasping for air.

A well-known comedian said he had no objection to death but he "didn't want to be there at the time." I find that a very funny line, but I totally disagree with it. If I have a choice, I want to be very aware of my dying and be conscious enough to cooperate with it. Death is my last trip, and I want to do it well.

On the day of my death, I would like to celebrate a simple Taoist Eucharist with bread and three cups in the morning with a few people. That would be my last meal. In the evening, along about twilight, I would like to be in a comfortable chair on the porch where I can watch the shadows lengthen and the evening come, and the busy world be hushed, and know that the fever of life is over and my work is done. I would like a safe lodging and peace at the last.

During my dying, I would like to have my closest loved ones around me and tell them one more time that I love them. Then I would recite one more time the Nunc Dimittis, "Lord, now lettest thou thy servant depart in peace according to thy word. . . ." in the version I memorized while serving at the 8 o'clock service when I was a young boy.

For final words, I find it hard to improve upon, "Into thy hands I commend my spirit." I would like to have a deep feeling of gratitude for the gift of life and praise to my Blessed Lord, who gives me life and then takes it away. I would like to be expressing thankfulness as I drop into the ocean of oblivion.

So that is my Plan A. Because I do not always get what I want in life, I am content to shift to Plan B or Plan C or some other.

That's my thinking and feeling as of this date of writing. I put these things down on paper hoping that they might prompt your own thoughts and feelings. If you could choose the date and circumstances of your death, how would you describe them?

What Happens to "Me" After I Die?

Death comes, and then what happens? It is my conviction that the pattern for living and dying can be clearly seen in the death of Jesus and his resurrection. Jesus is the prime example of how to be a human being. His life grows out of the seed of true humanity. The more we seek to understand his living and dying, the more our own life is enhanced. The likelihood is increased for our being more a part of the solution and less a part of the problem.

After Jesus died, he rose in his family, friends, and all who share in Christ's living Body. So what happens to "me" after I die? I am frequently asked whether I believe in reincarnation. In reply, I usually say that I am the reincarnation of my parents, Harold Butcher and Elizabeth Ford, along with all their forebears all the way back to the Big Bang. I also know what my reincarnation looks like and can introduce you to her. I am already reincarnated in Marie, my beloved daughter. Her genetic inheritance and the continuing influence from me and her mother give Marie the ongoing task of sorting out what is beneficial and useful for her, what might need to be set aside, and what still needs to be integrated in her own psyche, especially in those places where the work is not finished in mine. At this moment I can show you two generations of my reincarnation through my daughter and granddaughter. I am profoundly amazed at the interconnections between generations. The gift of life is passed from one generation to the next.

We also continue to exist through the family, friends, acquaintances, opponents, enemies, and everyone else whose lives we have touched, just as their lives touch and influence ours. We human beings belong to an enormous web of life and death in which we are part of one another directly, indirectly, profoundly, subtly, intentionally, and unintentionally. Even our times of apathy are part of the mix.

What effect are we having? It may be miniscule, but this is clear: when everything is tallied up, will our lives show each of us to have been more a part of the problem or part of the solution? I hope my life score comes out more on the positive side. This I know; I have been given much more than I can ever give back, no matter how hard I try.

Living Until We Die

What matters most is that we go ahead and live until we die. A bumper sticker reads, "The one who dies with the most toys wins." Apparently some people are dedicated to accumulating as much as they can for themselves. Do they not see the humor in this bumper sticker, which actually points up the folly of accumulation? You really cannot take it with you. However, all our choices add up to our leaving life either a little bit better or a little bit worse than we found it. Why not renounce selfishness and put our energies into making gifts back to the Mystery of life?

What is our task? To take as much out of life as we can? Or is it to put as much back into life as we can? We come from the earth, and we return to the earth. Go to an Ash Wednesday service. Kneel down and receive ashes on your forehead and hear again the ancient words, "Remember, you are dust and to dust you shall return."

I find those words tremendously reassuring. They remind me that I am from the earth, I belong to the earth, and I shall return to the earth. I am very much part of life. I shall be recycled. What a wonderful feeling of being connected to life! Ash Wednesday empowers me to get on with my living until I die.

Among the many people whose lives inspire mine is my mother, Elizabeth Ford Butcher, who lived until she died. I would like to do the same. I have a great feeling of passion and joy about Jesus, the Gospels, and all the Holy Scriptures. I hope this passion and joy is coming through these pages to you. My particular contribution is to research all the Holy Scriptures and teach from them both in books like this and in seminars that I lead.

Meanwhile, as I continue my living while anticipating my dying, I close this book with a prayer of Paul that can be very strengthening:

I bow my knees before the Father, from whom every family in heaven and on earth takes its name. I pray that, according to the riches of his glory, he may grant that you may be strengthened in your inner being with power through his Spirit, and that Christ may dwell in your hearts through faith, as you are being rooted and grounded in love. I pray that you may have the power to comprehend, with all the saints, what is the breadth and length and height and depth, and to know the love of Christ that surpasses knowledge, so that you may be filled with all the fullness of God.

Now to him who by the power at work within us is able to accomplish abundantly far more than all we can ask or imagine, to him be glory in the church and in Christ Jesus to all generations, forever and ever. Amen.

(Eph. 3:14–21, NRSV)

Conclusion
What, Then,
Is Resurrection?

Is resurrection historic truth? Is it mythic truth? Is it one or the other? Is it a blend of both? Questions like these run through our explorations into the meaning of the resurrection stories. A single sentence from *The Gospel of Philip* provides a way into the very heart of the matter: "Truth did not come into the world naked, but it came in types and images" (Gospel of Philip 67:9, NHL). As we have seen, symbol, myth, even outrageous stories all serve their purpose—to get our attention and assist us in finding our way into realities that defy description.

An introductory study of the written records reveals that there were, in the words of William James, as many varieties of resurrection experience in the first century as there are now in the twenty-first.

Sometimes the question is posed, "Do you believe in life after death?" A more immediate question is, "Do you believe in life after birth?" I believe in life after birth in a world where so many people seem to be walking around not really living their lives. They seem to be going through the motions or are too timid and too fearful to risk living and loving.

What makes the difference? How can one really live life? The way into life is through the life and teachings of Jesus continued through the Resurrected Jesus, who just happens to be very alive right now!

The following lines summarize rather well everything that I have been attempting to say in this book: "Do not think the resurrection is an illusion. It is no illusion, but it is truth. It is the revelation of what is, and the transformation of things, and a transition into newness" (The Treatise on Resurrection 48:10–38, NHL).

Appendix A
Virgin Birth Stories as Mythic Truth

When we look into the Gospel records of Jesus, we find that the earliest written Gospels, Thomas and Q, are collections of sayings attributed to Jesus with no information whatsoever about his life. Mark, the earliest of the narrative Gospels, does surround the teachings with other stories of Jesus' life, including healings, conflict with authorities, and the eventual trial, crucifixion, death, and resurrection; but in Mark, there is still no mention of the birth of Jesus.

The familiar nativity stories that many of us have known from childhood come from Matthew and Luke. There are additional Gospels with other versions of the nativity story. One of them is a second-century document called *The Gospel of James*. Our main sources are Matthew, Luke, and James. When you compare these three Gospels, you find some interesting similarities and some significant differences.

All the stories agree that Mary is a virgin. Luke says Mary is a "virgin engaged to a man whose name was Joseph" (Luke 1:27, NRSV). An angel says to Mary: "The Holy Spirit will come upon you, and the power of the Most High will overshadow you." Mary questions this and says, "How can this be, since I am a virgin?" The angel reassures her and then Mary says, "Let it be . . .". ; in that moment she conceives (Luke 34–38, NRSV).

The Gospel of Matthew spells out Mary's virginity even more clearly by saying: "Now the birth of Jesus Christ took place in this way. When his mother Mary had been betrothed to Joseph, before they came together she was found to be with child of the Holy Spirit" (Matt. 1:18, RSV).

In *The Gospel of James*, a woman named Salome doubts that Mary is a virgin, so she does a very graphic test: Salome "inserted her finger into Mary" (Gospel of James 20:2, SV) and discovers that Mary is still a virgin after delivering the child.

For many of us it is a stretch of our credulity to believe the virgin birth as a literal fact. Are we expected to stretch our imaginations even further to believe that her virginity was restored after the delivery?

Study the stories a bit more and compare what these three versions say regarding the place of birth: Luke says the Child is born in a stable with a manger for a bed; Matthew places the Holy Family in a house where the wise men visit; James uses a cave for the setting. So which is it: a stable, a house, or a cave?

Compare some of the other details: Luke says that an angel comes to Mary in the daytime; Matthew says that an angel appears to Joseph in his dreams. These are details that are easy to reconcile simply by saying that Mary heard the message during the day and Joseph heard it at night.

Luke says the angels brought their message to the shepherds in their fields at night. Matthew says the wise men followed a star and came with their gifts for the Child. You will find no shepherds in Matthew, no wise men in Luke.

These stories with very different details lived side by side until the thirteenth century when Francis of Assisi conflated the stories and created outdoors, where everyone could see, the first complete and full-size nativity scene: Holy Family with a live baby, shepherds, angels, wise men, and plenty of animals. The only missing character is King Herod, who is nowhere in sight.

Look at various crèches and nativity scenes on Christmas cards we have today, and once in a while you will see one where the scene is a cave with a stable inside. So if you work at it, you can reconcile most of the details into one somewhat coherent story.

Some choose to accept the story as a literal event in all detail and have no difficulty with the virgin birth, saying, "With God all things are possible." Others find a literal virgin birth difficult, if not impossible, to accept. In either case, certain questions remain. What do these stories really mean? What difference might they make in our lives now?

Consider the possibility that these stories might be true symbolically. They are myth in the best sense of that word. Sometimes we might have the impression that "myth" is another way of saying "not true, false." On the other hand, consider again one of Joseph Campbell's definitions: "Myth is a tale told to tell the truth."[1] Myth is a vehicle that conveys meaning to us. The truth is carried inside these extraordinary stories.

As you may know, virgin birth stories are found in other religious traditions. There are stories that say that the Buddha was born from his virgin mother Maya. In China, stories say that Lao Tsu and Confucius were also virgin born. This list of those who are said to be virgin born includes Zoroaster in Persia, Ra in Egypt, Prometheus, Plato, and even Alexander the Great in Greece, Romulus and Remus in Rome, and Quetzalcoatl in Mexico. There are virgin birth stories among the Mayans, Columbians, Nicaraguans, and many other cultures.

So what shall we make of all this information? Should we consider all these stories as literal historic fact? Or shall we say that only the Christian versions are historically true and all the others are false?

Suppose we accept the stories for their symbolic truth. Finding similar stories in so many cultures might be telling us that something very, very important is seeking expression through the stories.

Truth that is indescribable often clothes itself in outrageous stories, just to get our attention. They are designed to startle us and make us pay attention. Once the virgin birth stories get our attention, then we are ready to ask, "What in the world do they mean?"

Virgin birth stories are packed with meaning regarding who Jesus is. A human mother is impregnated by the Holy Spirit. Thus one of the things the stories are saying is that the divine comes fully into a human being.

Exploring the Inner Meaning of Virgin Birth Stories

Virgin birth stories also carry insight into the depths of our own spiritual lives. The Christmas carol "O Little Town of Bethlehem," written by Bishop Phillips Brooks, says it all in one line, "Be born in us today!" Consider the virgin birth stories as a symbolic description of our own inner rebirth.

Start with the place of birth: What might the three symbols of the stable, the house, and the cave suggest?

A stable is a very earthy, natural place. Do you have places in nature where God is especially real and present to you: a mountaintop, a forest, a desert, a waterfall, a tranquil lake, a special beach, or somewhere else?

Do you experience something of God's presence in your home, in your marriage, in your family, in a close friendship, with your lover? As you think about your significant relationships, now or at another time in your life, are there moments when you feel very deeply that the Divine is present and alive?

Consider the third symbol, a cave—a natural womb of the earth. There is within every human being that inner cavelike place where the Divine seeks to be born.

And where does this spiritual birth happen for us: in nature, in our relationships, in the depths of our souls, or in all of the above?

The nativity stories provide us with the symbolic clues we need. Have you ever looked at the stories and considered the possibility that all the characters might represent parts of ourselves?

Just as Mary is viewed as a virgin, there is also a virginal part within each of us. What might that virginal part be? The untouched part? The part that wants to be open to receive the Holy Spirit? The part that is wanting new life to be created from within? Might it even be the void within? Is there an emptiness yearning to be filled?

Such a place actually exists within us. Of course, we may be like Mary who asks, "How can this be?" We may question, we may doubt, and that questioning and doubting are a natural part of the process. When we are ready to hear it, the truth remains, quite simply and amazingly: the Divine is seeking to be born within us. You may know what this experience is. You may have received the baptism in the Holy Spirit. You may have experienced your own rebirth. There may be other ways in which the Divine is real to you.

If so, I suspect your experience may have come when you were especially vulnerable, receptive, and able to say, "Let it be!" The new birth can occur somewhere out in nature, or when we are very open and vulnerable to another person, or whenever we let go and allow God to enter us and touch our hearts.

Once the new birth has been conceived in us, there is a time of inner growth. Women who have become pregnant, carried a child for nine months, and given birth have a distinct advantage in understanding the process. Conception, pregnancy, and birth are an incredible Mystery and can be a deep spiritual experience for a woman.

In addition, this nine-month growth period is a symbol of the rebirth process that is possible for all of us, males as well as females. For example, both sexes can experience something new struggling to be born in the midst of a midlife crisis. But the newness is not restricted to midlife. It can happen at any age.

When we experience in ourselves something of the union with the Divine and the new birth has occurred, it is time for the friends to see the Child. The relatives come, and so do the shepherds and the wise ones. In this realization of new life there is a feeling of amazement and great exultation, a song in the heart. It is time to rejoice!

What might these figures represent? Joseph symbolizes that part of our-selves that serves as the protector of the mother and the Child that has just been born. He is attentive to what is going on and who is coming in and out of the place. Even at night he is alert because he pays attention to his dreams; he knows that they may contain the very information he needs for carrying out his task of protecting the new life from danger.

Shepherds live close to the earth. Symbolically, they care for our animals, our instinctual nature. So bring your naturalness, your instincts and desires to be with the Child. Look for those who are lost and are crying out to be found. They could be transformed with new power and energy.

Symbolically, the wise ones bring the treasures of the mind—your intellect and all your rational faculties. Let them come into relationship with the Child. Bring both your shepherds and your wise ones to that new holy center of your life and you may discover you are beginning to feel and think differently.

There is one character who is not usually portrayed in nativity scenes but is hidden away, King Herod. Consider what he might represent. A king has power, authority, and control. So why would a king be afraid of a baby? Maybe this baby will grow up and threaten the king. Nip the problem in the bud; kill the infant now if necessary.

There is no historical evidence of any king actually killing all these babies during the time when Jesus was born. But the symbolic truth remains. Change in the soul can be a threat to our inner power structure, the parts of ourselves that want to remain in control, the standard operating procedures that do not want to yield. Change is difficult; we resist and fight against it.

Whenever anyone has a spiritual breakthrough, he or she can anticipate an initial feeling of resolution and peace. Often this feeling is followed by a second reaction. For example, the person with a problem of drinking, drugs, gambling, or debt who has turned his life over to a higher power may first experience a feeling of great peace. Before long, the old forces and habits may come charging back and put up a fight. These forces, old patterns constellated in the symbol of Herod, do not want to be displaced.

The part of ourselves that provides inner law and order is necessary but needs to be transformed. Otherwise, it becomes dangerous to ourselves and to others. When the inner king lets go of his fears and comes to the child, not to kill it but to see what he might learn, then there is real movement toward wholeness.

Consider an example of spiritual rebirth—an unenlightened chief executive officer of a corporation for whom the bottom line is all that matters. A CEO can do some very unethical and destructive things, such as manipulating excessive salaries for himself while putting large numbers of people out of work and destroying any sense of loyalty to and from employees. Through decisions made by this CEO, the company might also exploit workers in other countries and cause serious ecological damage. Yet there is hope. An unethical CEO like this could have an experience of enlightenment and come to realize that besides the bottom line there are other considerations: trust, loyalty, consideration for employees, suppliers, and the environment, just to mention a few factors. After his coming into a new consciousness, will his old king, his old standard operating procedures, adjust easily, or are they likely to put up a fight first?

So is the virgin birth story true? Yes, it is very true! It describes our own inner spiritual process of rebirth. It is the story illustrating our own process toward enlightenment.

Take a moment and consider each of the characters in the story as parts of yourself: Is there a virginal Mary within you ready for something new? Is there a child waiting to be born? Might there be Joseph, the protector, with his dreams? Are you in touch with your shepherds, who have responsibility for guiding your instinctual animal energies? Are you acknowledging your wise ones with their treasures of the mind and intellect? Are there angels within carrying messages for you? Does your hidden King Herod have something to say? Is one of these characters in the story summoning your attention now?

I hope I have illustrated something of the tremendous value of the nativity stories. They carry at least two levels of mythic meaning: one presents, in symbolic language, the mystery of Jesus in whom the human and divine are fully integrated; the other provides the dynamics of our own spiritual rebirth.

It is my conviction that the nativity stories, the resurrection stories, and most stories in Holy Scripture contain both symbolic truth and historic truth. The two kinds of truth are woven together like the warp and woof in cloth. If the vertical strands in cloth are removed from the horizontal ones, the cloth falls apart and is lost. Instead of attempting to separate them from each other, why not enjoy the beauty of the whole cloth that Mystery is wearing?

Appendix B

Son of Man:
Seed of True Humanity

One of the most exciting discoveries in *The Gospel of Mary* is to find that the seed of the true humanity is at the very heart of the Gospel. The good news is that we can find our true selves and become more fully authentic human beings.

This phrase "seed of the true humanity" is also translated as the Son of Man, one of the most important concepts in the teachings of Jesus and also one of the least understood. I assume that most of us are accustomed to hearing the phrase "Son of God" applied to Jesus. Yet in his own vocabulary, he is much more likely to use the phrase "Son of Man." Trying to bring the message into understandable contemporary English is particularly difficult now because of the apparently one-sided sexist language in using the word "Son" and "Man."

Scholars have done significant research and have struggled with the problem of how to put into English a most significant Greek phrase, *ho huios tou anthropou*. Symptomatic of the difficulty is that at least one scholar devotes a major thesis to this phrase without ever translating it into English. Keeping the phrase in Greek may be appropriate for a doctoral thesis, but can be a stumbling block for the average person like myself, whose primary tongue in thought and speech is English.

Because most English translations of the phrase retain the use of "Son of Man," I will stick with that awkward phrase. I apologize to any and all who find the phrase offensive and ask you to hear with me. If we can crack this oyster, I believe we will find a magnificent pearl inside.

Jesus spoke Aramaic. The Gospels were written originally in Greek or Syriac. *The Gospel of Mary* was translated into Coptic and then, for our benefit, was translated into English. Going from Aramaic to Greek or Syriac into Coptic and then into English is a long trip for a potent phrase. Has it been battered in the journey?

To make the matter even more complex, Jesus never defines either of his two most important terms, "Son of Man" and "Kingdom of God." He tells us that the Kingdom of God is like yeast that a woman hides in bread, like treasure buried in a field, like a grain of mustard seed, like a woman with a leaking jar, and many other metaphors. It is like this. It is like that. Ask Jesus to define it, and he will give you yet another "It is like. . . ."

Is Jesus just being difficult? Because he is a teacher hoping that his students will understand, I doubt that he deliberately obscures what he has to say. I suspect that Jesus is up against limitations of the language of the first century, which lacks the vocabulary needed to express what he has discovered, knows, and feels. In some instances this seems to be the case.

We live in the twenty-first century, and the good news is that we have some helpful language unavailable to Jesus. For example, Jesus says, "Why do you see the speck in your neighbor's eye, but do not notice the log in your own eye?" (Luke 6:41, NRSV). Today we identify this process as "psychological projection," a phrase not available to Jesus in the language of his time. Jesus identifies the process of projection with his teachings about the eye coupled with his frequent phrase, "Do you have eyes, and fail to see?" (Mark 8:18, NRSV). Essentially, Jesus knows that our projections can blind our vision.

Beyond the limitation of language lies an even deeper problem. Jesus is dealing with the ultimate Mystery that defies definition. I suspect that when Jesus risks entering into the fullness of the Mystery, he, like anyone who has been in those holy depths, comes out speechless, stammering, unable to put the experience into words.

I hope this gives you a feeling for the problem we are facing in regard to the phrase "Son of Man." I believe there is a way out of the dilemma, and that is simply to begin by looking carefully at some of the places where Jesus uses "Son of Man." As we go through them, we may get a feeling and an understanding, even though we, like Jesus, may not be able to form an adequate definition.

Son of Man and Dry Bones Resurrecting

Jesus did not invent the phrase "Son of Man"; it had been around for centuries. The phrase appears ninety-three times in the Book of Ezekiel, for example.[1]

In the book that bears his name, Ezekiel hears a voice speaking to him and saying, "Son of man, stand upon your feet, and I will speak with you." Then Ezekiel says, "And when he spoke to me, that Spirit entered into me and set me upon my feet; and I heard him speaking to me" (Ezek. 2:1–2, RSV).

This is like the drill sergeant shouting "Attention!" and everyone jumps to his or her feet, stands at attention, and is ready to hear the next command and follow it precisely. It may also be like the Dalai Lama or Thich Nhat Hanh or any genuine spiritual master who says very gently, yet just as forcefully, "Pay attention!" Can you hear this command and the urgency to become fully aware?

Being addressed as "Son of Man" calls up the best in us. It reaches deeply behind all our facades into the core of our being to bring out our full potential. It is a call to be fully human. We are all ordinary human beings. The call to stand on our feet and bring forth our Son of Man quality is a call to be extraordinary human beings.

When the Holy Voice calls Ezekiel to attention, it gives him the message that he is responsible for conveying to the people. In the second chapter of the book, Ezekiel is called to be a watchman. Like a watchman or sentry on a tower, he is under orders to have his eyes peeled, his ears attuned to every sound, and a readiness to warn the people of any approaching danger.

If Ezekiel sees the danger, warns the people, and they do not pay attention to the message, then the blood of the forthcoming disaster is on their heads. But if Ezekiel hears the message and fails to warn the people, then the blood is on his head.

When I was ordained priest by Bishop Arthur Barksdale Kinsolving II in Trinity Episcopal Cathedral, Phoenix, Arizona, the preacher was my friend and priest, the Rev. David Churchman Trimble. He took as his text the second chapter of Ezekiel with this overwhelming message. I was addressed as "Son of Man" and called to be a responsible watchman. The message about the blood being on the heads of the people or on my head has left me continually sorting out questions of responsibility. Which responsibilities are mine, and which ones remain with others?

The exhortation and vow that I took from *The Book of Common Prayer*, 1928, calls me to be a "Messenger, watchman, and steward of the Lord"; it has a strength requiring commitment strong as steel. I was twenty-four years old when I heard the sermon and took the vow; I still feel the power of hearing the words, "Son of Man, you are called to be a watchman!"

I have illustrated from my own experience hoping that you may also feel the strength of being called to stand up on your feet, bring forth the fullness of your humanity, and be a responsible person, listening to the Holy Voice and acting on it.

One of the strongest messages of the Book of Ezekiel is about resurrection. This message was first delivered about six hundred years before the resurrection of Jesus.

You will need a vivid imagination for this one. Ezekiel is a seer with vision. A seer is one who really sees, not with the naked eye but with the naked heart. In his vision Ezekiel sees a valley filled with dry, sun-parched human bones. There has been a massive slaughter in the past, and now there is no life—just dry bones, wind swirling the dust, and silence.

The vision is an expression of what has happened to the people of Israel; Jerusalem has been captured and destroyed. The leadership and many of the people have been taken into exile in Babylon. The people are devastated, and the heart has been taken out of them.

The Voice asks Ezekiel a question, "Son of man, can these bones live?" And Ezekiel replies wisely, "O Lord GOD, thou knowest." Then the Voice calls to Ezekiel, "Prophesy to these bones, and say to them, O dry bones , hear the word of the LORD. Thus says the Lord GOD to these bones: Behold, I will cause breath to enter you, and you shall live. I will lay sinews upon you, and will cause flesh to come upon you, and cover you with skin, and put breath in you, And you shall live; and you shall know that I am the LORD" (Ezek. 37:3–6, RSV).

Ezekiel does as he is commanded; he calls loudly to the bones and watches as the bones respond. Suddenly there is a noise, a rattling, and the bones come together, bone to its bone, forming skeletons. The old spiritual, "Dem bones, dem bones, dem Dry Bones, now hear the Word of the Lord" is based in this scene.

Ezekiel continues watching as sinews form on the bones, then flesh, and then the skin. Now we see complete bodies, but they are only corpses with no life in them.

The Voice calls to Ezekiel again, saying, "Prophesy to the breath, prophesy, son of man, and say to the breath, Thus says the Lord GOD: Come from the four winds, O breath, and breathe upon these slain, that they may live" (Ezek. 37:9, RSV).

Ezekiel prophesies as he has been commanded, and the bodies live and stand on their feet, a vast multitude.

The immediate meaning is apparent. The vision speaks to the people who have been devastated. This vision still speaks to both individuals and groups. Out of devastation comes hope when the Son of Man is called forth to speak the word of the Lord.

To those who are sleepwalking through life, the call is "Wake Up!" To those who are apathetic, the call is, "Get up off your apathy!" To all who are numbed, dazed, only partially alert, the call is "Stand up, Son of Man!"

Son of Man Alive in Jesus and His Teaching

Jesus knows the Ezekiel stories and the many others from the Hebrew Scriptures. Jesus has heard the Voice calling him to stand upon his feet and speak the Word of the Lord. Jesus is in touch with his authentic humanity and lives out his "Son of Man" potential.

Many scenes illustrate how Jesus lives this out. In one of them, Jesus is at home in Capernaum. People are gathering in the house and crowding around the door to hear what he has to say. Four people come toward the house carrying a paralyzed friend on a mat that serves as a makeshift stretcher. There is no way to get into the house because of the crowd, so the four friends remove the tiles from the roof and lower their friend down into the house in front of Jesus. When Jesus sees their faith, he says to the paralytic, "Son, your sins are forgiven . . . Stand up and take up your mat and walk" (Mark 2:5, 9).

Is Jesus, like Ezekiel, speaking from his own Son of Man authority that enables the old bones of the paralytic to stand up and walk? Could it be that when Jesus says "Son," his voice calls forth the man's own Son of Man within so that he has the strength to stand up and walk? Might "Son of Man" be activated in both Jesus and the man who is freed of his paralysis in the encounter?

Paralysis takes many forms besides the literal. When someone says, "I just can't forgive him," healing of the hurt is needed so that there can be forgiveness and reconciliation. When someone faces a job interview or some other "impossible task" and feels immobilized, it is time to awaken the strength of one's true humanity to rise to the occasion.

In another scene it is a Sabbath day. Jesus and his disciples are walking through grainfields and begin plucking heads of grain, rubbing them in their hands, and eating them. Pharisees notice what they are doing. Even though the actions of the disciples may seem ordinary and harmless enough, the Pharisees interpret this as work that is forbidden on the Sabbath.

In one version, the Pharisees complain to Jesus saying, "Look, why are they doing what is not lawful on the sabbath?" (Mark 2:24, NRSV). In another version they accost Jesus himself saying, "Why are you doing what is not lawful on the sabbath?" (Luke 6:2, NRSV).

Jesus replies, "Have you not read what David did when he and his companions were hungry? He entered the house of God and took and ate the bread of the Presence, which is not lawful for any but the priests to eat, and gave some to his companions?" (Luke 6:3–4, NRSV).

While the Pharisees are thinking this one over, Jesus says, "The Son of Man is lord of the sabbath" (Luke 6:5, NRSV). What is Jesus really saying? Is he teaching that the authority of the Son of Man takes priority over the laws?

And who is this Son of Man? Is he to be identified only with Jesus? Or is the Son of Man that true humanity residing within everyone and needing to be actualized?

In the story, it is not just Jesus but his disciples as well who operate from this Son of Man authority that takes precedence over law in a specific situation. Law-and-order folks of any age or culture have trouble with this one.

Does this mean that the Son of Man is above the law? Or free to reinterpret the law? Or living from a deeper law?

A good friend of mine, Charles Brandon, sees in the Gospels an evolution of Jesus' own consciousness. For example, earlier in his ministry Jesus says things like, "Do not think that I have come to abolish the law or the prophets; I have come not to abolish but to fulfill" (Matt. 5:17, NRSV). Then scenes like this one in the grainfield and others occur. Later in his ministry Jesus says, "I give you a new commandment, that you love one another" (John 13:34, NRSV). Along the Way, Jesus discovers how to live out his Son of Man, which springs from the primary commandments to love the Lord with heart, soul, mind, and energy, and one's neighbor as oneself.

Another Son of Man passage is found in this scene from *The Q Gospel*. Jesus says, "How shall I describe the people of this generation? What are they like? They are like children who sit in the marketplace and call to one another: 'We played the flute for you and you didn't dance; we sang songs and you would not weep'" (The Q Gospel 26). (We played wedding and you wouldn't play; we played funeral and you wouldn't play. What *do* you want to play?)

John the Baptist came, not eating bread, not drinking wine, and you said, "He is crazy." Now the Son of Man comes, eating and drinking, and you say, "Just look at him, a glutton and a drunkard, a friend of tax collectors and outcasts." But Wisdom is being proven right by all her children (The Q Gospel 26).

The ministry of Jesus takes places in a variety of situations. You will find him in the marketplace with ordinary working people one moment and having dinner with officials the next. He is comfortable with respectable people in their homes and with prostitutes on the street. He goes to parties and drinks socially. He associates with those who don't know where their next meal is coming from. Women as well as men travel with him throughout his ministry. How is he able to move with such apparent ease among all sorts and conditions of people? Might this be, as Jesus suggests, the Son of Man energy operating from within him?

Some interpreters might attempt to identify "Son of Man" with Jesus and Jesus only. But the evidence is clear; Son of Man was lived out before Jesus in people like Ezekiel and after his death in people like Mary Magdalene, his brother James, and a host of others. I would include Mohandas K. Gandhi, Eleanor Roosevelt, Martin Luther King Jr., Dorothy Day, Mother Teresa, Remedios Varo, Nelson Mandela, Caesar Chavez, and Howard Zinn. "Son of Man," the energy of the authentic human being, is in every person waiting to be awakened and lived. It might be paralyzed, but it can be released and set free.

Jesus teaches what is involved in activating the Son of Man within us. For example, consider this saying from Jesus, "When you make the two one, you will become the sons of man . . ." (Gospel of Thomas 106, NHL). What might Jesus mean, "making the two one"?

Jesus says, "When you make the two one, and when you make the inside like the outside and the outside like the inside, and the above like the below, and when you make the male and the female one and the same, so that the male not be male nor the female female; and when you fashion eyes in place of an eye, and a hand in place of a hand, and a foot in place of a foot, and a likeness in place of a likeness; then you will enter the Kingdom" (Gospel of Thomas 22, NHL).

So is that all perfectly clear? Sometimes the teachings of Jesus resemble Zen koans such as, "What is the sound of one hand clapping?" You simply have to meditate on the teaching for a while, start living it out, then you will discover what it really means.

I do not pretend to grasp fully the meaning of *The Gospel of Thomas* 22. However, the insights of Carl Gustav Jung give me some clues, particularly as regards the male and female. If men have within them their anima (feminine energy) and women have within them their animus (masculine energy), then the challenge is to discover how to integrate the opposites.

In broad sweeps, this means getting your trip together—both the outer trip and the inner trip. I have a good friend who once took a sledge hammer to her house and knocked out inner walls before beginning the process of restoring a fine old house. In a very real sense she has also taken a sledge hammer to her inner house, knocking out old walls and barriers; now she is in the process of restoring her inner life. Her inner world and her outer world are playing off each other. In due course, both will come into greater synchronicity.

In Luke there is a scene where Jesus is speaking, and a man named Zacchaeus, who happens to be a tax collector, is eager to see Jesus and hear what he is teaching. The problem is that the crowd is big and Zacchaeus is short. Zacchaeus scrambles up a tree where he can get a better view. Jesus spots him and says, "Zacchaeus, hurry up and climb down; I have to stay at your house today" (Luke 19:5, SV). Jesus is criticized for associating with a tax collector, rather like having dinner with a member of the Internal Revenue Service. After hearing Jesus' teachings, Zacchaeus says, "Look, sir, I'll give half of what I own to the poor, and if I have extorted anything from anyone, I'll pay back four times as much." Jesus replies, "Today salvation has come to this house. This man is a real son of Abraham" (Luke 19:8–9, SV). Then comes the punch line, "For the Son of Man came to seek out and to save the lost" (Luke 19:10, NRSV).

And what is lost? Are there lost or missing parts of ourselves needing to be found and integrated? One function of the Son of Man within us is to seek out and save the lost, as in Jesus' parables of the shepherd looking for the lost sheep, the woman looking for the lost coin, and the father looking for the lost son (Luke 15).

Jesus says, "The foxes have their holes and the birds have their nests, but the Son of Man has no place to lay his head and rest" (Gospel of Thomas 86 and The Q Gospel 27).

Does this mean that anyone functioning from the true humanity within will be homeless? After his baptism, Jesus moves about a great deal. People who decide to "follow him" literally give up what they are doing and go on the road with him. Will we all become vagabonds? Or is Jesus speaking about a spirit of detachment here? On other occasions Jesus has spoken about losing one's life to find it. For example, he counsels a rich man to sell all and give to the poor.

Jesus often speaks in paradox, and it becomes clear that once you give up everything, really let go, then all is given back to you. Like so many teachings of Jesus, they must be lived to be understood.

Toward the end of his ministry, we hear Jesus making statements about the Son of Man being betrayed and having to endure suffering. Jesus pays the price of living according to his true humanity. We know the results.

And what about us? It is one thing to seek out and live our true humanity. We may even be willing to be a bit countercultural in the process. How far are we willing to go in living our true humanity? What if it involves being betrayed, having friends desert us, enduring suffering, losing everything, and dying a miserable death?

Even after the death of Jesus, the gospel of the Son of Man, the seed of the true humanity, persists. As we have already seen, it is carried by Mary Magdalene, who gives her own clear voice to the message of the Resurrected Jesus.

The Voice who spoke to Ezekiel, Jesus, the paralyzed man, and Mary Magdalene persists in saying things like this to us, "Son of Man, Daughter of Humanity, stand up on your feet, listen to my Voice. Speak and act out of your true humanity. The seed is already within you, so let it sprout, take root, and grow!"

Appendix C
Mary Magdalene's Dialogue with Her Soul

The Gospel of Mary 9 contains the last portion of a dialogue between Mary Magdalene and her soul. The first four pages of the dialogue are missing. The material that remains is spiritually very deep and may be difficult to follow. It may become clear only after we have entered into the experiences she describes. Here is what she writes.

> Desire says, "I did not see you go down, yet now I see you go up. So why do you lie since you belong to me?" The soul answers, "I saw you. You did not see me nor did you know me. You mistook the garment I wore for my true self. And you did not recognize me"
>
> (Gospel of Mary 9:2–5, SV).

As I read these lines I recall immediately a line from another conversation: "[Human beings] look on the outward appearance, but the LORD looks on the heart" (I Sam. 16:7, NRSV).

Jesus says, "When you make the two into one, and when you make the inner like the outer, and the upper like the lower, and when you make the male and female into a single one. . . then you will enter into the kingdom of the Father" (Gospel of Thomas 22, SV).

One person is strongly attracted to another and may even feel a very deep connection. The other may feel the same way. Or the other may object and say, "But you don't know me!" How clearly do we really see one another?

When are we seeing clearly? When are we projecting? When are two people blinded by their mutual projections? The issues of perception and projection are illustrated in this conversation between the heart's desire and the soul, who says the same thing in three ways:

1. "You did not see me nor did you know me"
2. "You mistook the garment I wore for my true self"
3. "You did not recognize me"

Once the issue is so clearly identified, an interesting thing happens. The story says that "after it had said these things, the soul left rejoicing greatly" Unmasking the projection by naming it creates freedom and rejoicing.

The dialogue continues with each of seven forms of power:

"The first form is Darkness; the second, Desire; the third, Ignorance; the fourth, Zeal for Death; the fifth the Domain of the Flesh; the sixth, the Foolish Wisdom of the Flesh; the seventh, the Wisdom of the Wrathful Person" (Gospel of Mary 9:18–24, SV).

What does the soul do with each of these forms of power? The soul could avoid them, ignore them, hope they will go away on their own accord. But the soul actually faces and confronts each of these dark energies and in so doing they lose their grip and power over the soul.

Greater understanding may come by counting the powers down from the seventh to the first. The seventh is the wrathful power, the wrathful part of ourselves. Underneath the anger and wrath might be found hurt that needs healing. There might be an ego that needs to give up being egocentric and find its true center. Anger is often the symptom of something deeper. Once there is dialogue with the core issue, then out of the wrathful person comes wisdom.

The sixth and fifth forms of power have to do with the flesh. Dialogue with the flesh may reveal and unmask its foolish wisdom and its dominance over us. In the process, the soul becomes free.

It is likewise with the fourth, zeal for death. The lion's share of the national budget of the United States of America is an investment in death. The military industrial complex and the Central Intelligence Agency tax the brains, energy, and money of the people to invest in death, war, and better ways to kill whoever is seen to be the enemy. When will we as a country and as individuals have the courage to face this zeal for death, unmask it, see what lies behind it, and redirect the energies into life?

When the masks come off, what do we find? Are there deep-seated fears that need to be faced? Is our national shadow being projected onto other people? Are powerful business interests trying to justify their weapons design and production?

The third form of power is ignorance in all its forms. How is ignorance overcome? Knowledge and wisdom are the answer, not just information. It is commonplace these days to recognize that we have an information glut. Information technologies have spun out of control. When will we learn how to use information wisely?

The second is desire. How will we deal with desire? Will we allow desire full expression with no controls whatsoever? Will we attempt to kill it before it can do any damage? Will we ignore it and hope it will go away? Or might we enter dialogue with it so that it might be transformed?

Jesus gives us a brief but potent prayer that contains the phrase "Thy will be done." Behind this English phrase is the Greek and behind that is the

Aramaic language that Jesus most likely spoke. Start freshly with the Aramaic, translate it directly into English, and we get, "Thy heart's desire be done."[1] What might be the heart's desire of the Father, the Source of all we call "God"? We may seek to bring our will into conformity with the will of the Father. On the other hand, our task may be to bring our desires into relationship with the ultimate heart's desire. In that holy relationship our souls can be set free.

We are moving into the deepest level now, darkness, which is why I suggested the countdown from the seventh to the primary power of darkness.

So often darkness is considered to be not only negative, but evil, and something to be avoided at all cost. Yet the Creation story reveals that it is out of the darkness that light comes. Without darkness, where could light originate?

Once the soul dialogues with each and every level of the powers, then the soul can say, "What binds me has been slain, and what surrounds me has been destroyed, and my desire has been brought to an end and my ignorance has died" (Gospel of Mary 9:27, SV).

The soul has a choice, either to try to eliminate the powers or to discover how to transform them. A teaching from Jesus illustrates this choice:

> "When the unclean spirit has gone out of a person, it wanders through waterless regions looking for a resting place, but it finds none. Then it says, 'I will return to my house from which I came.' When it comes, it finds it empty, swept, and put in order. Then it goes and brings along seven other spirits more evil than itself, and they enter and live there; and the last state of that person is worse than the first."
>
> (Matt. 12:43–45, NRSV)

Jesus warns us about the risk of ejecting an unclean spirit without hearing what the spirit has to say. When the unclean spirit is not acknowledged, not heard, and not understood, its anger escalates. The unclean spirit leaves only to gather up its cronies and return.

Often good resolutions alone are ineffective when the underlying issues have not been recognized. Cleaning up your act requires dealing with the issues behind the mess.

Jesus, in his own life, demonstrates a creative way to deal with the powers. For example, during his wilderness experience after his baptism, Jesus engages Satan in dialogue. Through those conversations the powers are disarmed. Having been heard, they depart of their own accord.

The soul, having first confronted the powers, is now able to say, "From now on, for the rest of the course of the (due) measure of the time of the age, I will rest in silence" (Gospel of Mary 9:29, SV). When Mary finishes relaying her dialogue with her soul, she falls silent.

Appendix D

Comparing the Teachings
of James and Jesus

After Jesus died, his followers spoke and wrote in his name. When were their teachings consistent with his? When did they expand on what he had to say? And when did they diverge from what he taught? These questions are not easily answered because we have nothing whatsoever in writing from Jesus himself. Comparisons are a challenging and worthwhile study because they may reveal how the teaching evolved in new contexts.

In searching for the consistencies and inconsistencies between the teachings of Jesus and those of his followers, a case in point is a comparative study of the teachings of Jesus and James.

We have one written document that many scholars accept as coming from James or from his followers. It is a short letter known as the Letter of James and is included in the New Testament. A fascinating study is to compare the Letter of James with the teachings of Jesus as recorded in the Gospels.

Probably the most noticeable are the correlations between the teaching of James and the collection of Jesus' teachings called the Sermon on the Mount found in Matthew 5—7.

Some sayings of James are almost identical with those of Jesus. For example, James says, "Do not swear by heaven or by earth or use any oaths at all. If you mean 'yes', you must say 'yes'; if you mean 'no', say 'no. Otherwise you make yourself liable for judgment" (James 5:12, NJB). Compare this with what Jesus says: "Do not swear at all, either by heaven, since that is God's throne, or by the earth, since that is his footstool; or by Jerusalem, since that is the city of the great king. Do not swear by your own head either, since you cannot turn a single hair white or black. All you need say is 'Yes' if you mean yes, 'No' if you mean no; anything more than this comes from the evil one" (Matt. 5:34–37, JB).

Might James have received this saying from Jesus? On the other hand, might Jesus have received it from James? Might either or both of them have learned it from experience?

Being able to say a clear "Yes" or "No" reminds me of a story Jesus tells, "What do you think? A man had two sons; he went to the first and said, 'Son, go and work in the vineyard today.' He answered, 'I will not'; but later he changed his mind and went. The father went to the second and said the same; and he answered, 'I go sir'; but he did not go. Which of the two did the will of his father?" (Matt. 21:28–31, NRSV).

For many years, when I read this story I would mentally answer Jesus' question with "the first son" and move on. But the day came when I was at Four Springs just outside Middletown, California, participating in a seminar on *The Records of Jesus* led by Elizabeth Howes, founder of the Guild for Psychological Studies. We began to explore the dynamic within this story in terms of "No" and "Yes."

One brother's initial response is to say "No" to his father's request. Then he changes his mind and through his action his response becomes a clear "Yes."

The other brother's initial response is "Yes." He, too, changes his mind to a "No" by simply not doing anything.

For those of us who usually respond "Yes," what are we doing? Trying to please? Trying to be cooperative? Not wanting to let anyone down? Afraid to say "No"?

If there are times when someone agrees to do something and somehow it just never happens, what is really going on? Might there have already been a "No" somewhere inside that person?

The world is full of "Yes" people, and the world is full of "No" people. There are some whose first response to a request is usually "No." What might be some of the reasons for saying "No" at first: not wanting to get involved, trying to create some time to think it over, or some other reason?

What enables an initial "No" to become a "Yes"?

Paying attention to our first response in a given situation and then asking ourselves if there might be a second response behind it will enable us to be in touch with our feelings, work them through, and come to a clear answer we can act upon. Essentially, both Jesus and James are teaching us to make a good, clear, clean, honest response, whether it is affirmative or negative.

Another place where James and Jesus have almost identical teachings occurs when James asks why blessing and cursing come out of the same mouth. Then he adds: "My brothers and sisters, this ought not to be so. Does a spring pour forth from the same opening both fresh and brackish water? Can a fig tree, my brothers and sisters, yield olives or a grapevine figs? No more can salt water yield fresh" (James 3:10–12, NRSV).

Jesus, in speaking about false prophets, says, "You will know them by their fruits. Are grapes gathered from thorns, or figs from thistles? In the same way, every good tree bears good fruit, but the bad tree bears bad fruit" (Matt. 7:16–17, NRSV).

Both James and Jesus call our attention to inconsistent behavior and warn about hypocrisy. The root meaning of "hypocrite" is to be an actor. There is nothing wrong with being an actor on stage, film, or video when everyone knows the actor is playing an assigned role. However, in daily living, when someone is only acting and not being authentic, then hypocrisy is at work.

Jesus goes deeper than James by citing the root cause of hypocrisy, a heart that needs changing. Jesus is clear in his teachings that it is the heart that needs transformation. The more I read James and the more I read Jesus, the more I sense that James addresses behavior whereas Jesus goes much deeper to the causes of the behavior. "The Kingdom is inside of you, and it is outside of you. When you come to know yourselves, then you will become known, and you will realize that it is you who are the sons of the living Father" (Gospel of Thomas 3, NHL). Moreover, "When you make the two one, and when you make the inside like the outside and the outside like the inside . . . then you will enter the Kingdom" (Gospel of Thomas 22, NHL).

How do we move toward greater consistency between our behavior and what is already within us? Jesus provides the clue; it is knowing our relationship with the Father, that is, with God, the Source of Life. When the Spirit of the Father is moving within us, then we will produce the fruits of that Spirit.

The more closely our inner spirit is lived in relationship with the Source of Life, the more consistent and less hypocritical will be our behavior. In addition, we are more likely to find ourselves in conflict with some of the prevailing attitudes in our society.

James understands the conflicts and the potential suffering and writes, "My brothers and sisters, consider it a great joy when trials of many kinds come upon you, for you well know that the testing of your faith produces perseverance, and perseverance must complete its work so that you will become fully developed, complete, not deficient in any way" (James 1:2–4, NJB). A little later he writes even more succinctly, "Blessed is anyone who perseveres when trials come" (James 1:12, NJB).

Might these sayings be an echo of Jesus saying, "Blessed are those who are persecuted for righteousness' sake, for theirs is the kingdom of heaven" (Matt. 5:10, NRSV)?

In his Beatitudes, Jesus says, "Blessed are you who are poor, for yours is the kingdom of God" (Luke 6:20, NRSV). James alludes to this when he writes, "Listen, my dear brothers and sisters: it was those who are poor according to the world that God chose to be rich in faith and to be the heirs to the kingdom which he promised to those who love him" (James 2:5, NJB).

James extends even further the teachings of Jesus when he writes:

"Do not let class distinctions enter into your faith in Jesus Christ, our glorified Lord. Now suppose a man comes into your synagogue, well dressed and with a gold ring on, and at the same time a poor man comes in, in shabby clothes, and you take notice of the well-dressed man, and say, 'Come this way to the best seats'; then you tell the poor man, 'Stand over there' or 'You can sit on the floor by my footrest.' In making this distinction among yourselves, have you not used a corrupt standard?"

(James 2:1–4, NJB).

Reading these lines, my mind immediately recalls Jesus' story of the rich man and the poor man at his gate (Luke 16:19–31).

I could cite more examples in comparing the teachings of James with those of his brother, Jesus. I hope these few have whetted your appetite to do some research on your own. You, too, can open up James and make your own comparisons with the teachings of Jesus in the Gospels. When you do, be sure to work with all five of the Gospels: Thomas, Mark, Matthew, Luke, and John. The more I read James and compare his message with that of Jesus in the Gospels, the greater similarities I see.

Jesus and James on Healing

Jesus is known for his teaching and for his ministry of healing. Also, he commissions his disciples, to share in healing ministry, saying, "Go, preach, saying, the kingdom of heaven is at hand. Heal the sick, cleanse the lepers, raise the dead, cast out devils: freely ye have received, freely give" (Matt. 10:7–8, KJV). Likewise, James writes, "Anyone who is in trouble should pray; anyone in good spirits should sing a psalm. Any one of you who is ill should send for the elders of the church, and they must anoint the sick person with oil in the name of the Lord and pray over him. The prayer of faith will save the sick person and the Lord will raise him up again; and if he has committed any sins, he will be forgiven" (James 5:13–15, NJB).

Both Jesus and James were men of prayer. James writes, "Prayer must be made with faith, and no trace of doubt" (James 1:6, NJB). How similar this is to Jesus' teaching: "If you do not doubt in your heart, but believe that what you say will come to pass, it will be done for you. So I tell you, whatever you ask for in prayer, believe that you have received it, and it will be yours" (Mark 11:23–24, NRSV).

In healings, Jesus uses prayer, touch, and sometimes anointing with clay and spittle. Even though there is no specific reference to Jesus' anointing with oil, Mark tells us that the twelve "anointed with oil many who were sick and cured them" (Mark 6:13, NRSV).

Oil is a symbol of the Holy Spirit, who provides healing and renewed energy. In the Hebrew Scriptures, prophets anointed with oil those who were to become kings. In the Gospels, Mary Magdalene anoints Jesus and empowers him to face whatever is ahead of him. Renewing power is conveyed through the prayerful energy accompanying the oil and the touching. The anointing with oil releases reservoirs of trust and faith from within.

Somewhere in the process there is trust, faith. In the healing stories, faith functions in several different ways. A woman approaches Jesus saying to herself, "If I but touch his clothes, I will be made well" (Mark 5:28, NRSV). When she touches him, Jesus asks, "Who touched my clothes?" (Mark 5:30, NRSV). As Jesus looks around to see who has drawn energy from him, the woman comes to him and tells the whole truth. Turning toward her, Jesus says, "Daughter, your faith has made you well" (Mark 5:34, NRSV). She has the faith and the initiative that releases the healing power like a switch turning on the current.

In other situations, it appears that it is the faith of one person that enables the healing of another, as with the centurion asking in faith for the healing of his servant. (Matt. 8:5–13). In the story of the paralyzed man, four friends carry him on a stretcher to Jesus. Their faith is so strong that when they cannot get into the house because of the crowd, they carry the stretcher up onto the roof, make an opening in the roof, and lower the man down to Jesus. The faith of the friends is a significant part of the healing process.

In the healing of the man born blind, the word *faith* does not occur, but is clearly demonstrated by action. After anointing the man's eyes with clay, Jesus says, "Go, wash in the pool of Siloam. . . . Then he went and washed and came back able to see" (John 9:7, NRSV).

James says, "It is by my deeds that I will show you my faith" (James 2:18, NJB). The saying "Actions speak louder than words" would be very much in harmony with how James lived his life.

Notice what James adds when he writes about healing; he says, "send for the elders of the church." The word "church" comes from the Greek word *ecclesia*, meaning an "assembly." People today who gather and call themselves "The Assembly of God" are right on target. Yet the word *ecclesia* does not occur in the vocabulary of Jesus. The two exceptions in the Gospels relate to the saying about Peter and building the church (Matt. 16:18) and to the instruction regarding settling an argument between brothers (Matt. 18:15–18). Most scholars agree that these two sayings are not from Jesus but were added later. Jesus was too busy moving about to have a settled assembly anywhere.

James served as high priest for an assembly in Jerusalem that would have already had leaders, or elders, in place. These faith-filled people became part of the healing process for others.

Appendix E
Thomas the Contender

When exploring the question of continuities and discontinuities between the teachings of Jesus and later experiences of the Resurrected Jesus, we find a fascinating study in *The Book of Thomas the Contender*, a third-century document found in the Nag Hammadi Library in a Coptic translation that probably originated in Edessa, Syria. Its teachings are presented in the form of a resurrection conversation between the Risen Christ and his twin brother Judas Thomas.

Looking for continuities between these teachings in *The Book of Thomas the Contender* and those of the historic Jesus, one might notice the similarity in literary form in the Beatitudes. Jesus is recorded as saying:

"Blessed are the poor, for yours is the Kingdom of Heaven."
(Gospel of Thomas 54, NHL)

"Blessed are you who are poor, for yours is the Kingdom of God.
"Blessed are you who are hungry now, for you will be filled.
"Blessed are you who weep now, for you will laugh."
(Luke 6:20–21, NRSV)

"Blessed are the merciful, for they will receive mercy.
"Blessed are the pure in heart, for they will see God.
"Blessed are the peacemakers, for they will be called children of God.
"Blessed are those who are persecuted for righteousness' sake,
for theirs is the kingdom of heaven."
(Matt. 5:7–9, NRSV)

"Blessed are they who have been persecuted within themselves.
It is they who have truly come to know the Father."
(Gospel of Thomas 69, NHL)

"Blessed is the man who has suffered and found life."
(Gospel of Thomas 58 NHL)

Similar teachings are now attributed to the Resurrected Jesus in The Book of Thomas the Contender:

"Blessed is the wise man who sought after the truth, and when he found it, he rested upon it forever and was unafraid of those who wanted to disturb him."
(Thomas the Contender 140:42, NHL)

"Blessed are you who have prior knowledge of the stumbling blocks and who flee alien things.
"Blessed are you who are reviled and not esteemed on account of the love their Lord has for them.
"Blessed are you who weep and are oppressed by those without hope, for you will be released from every bondage."
(Thomas the Contender 145:2–8, NHL)

The other side of the "Blesseds" are the "Woes." Jesus is recorded as saying:

"Woe to you who are rich, for you have received your consolation.
"Woe to you who are full now, for you will be hungry.
"Woe to you who laughing now, for you will mourn and weep.
"Woe to you when all speak well of you, for that is what their ancestors did to the false prophets."
(Luke 6:24–26, NRSV)

In *The Book of Thomas the Contender*, we find these sayings attributed to the Resurrected Jesus.

"Woe to you who hope in the flesh and in the prison that will perish! How long will you be oblivious? And the imperishables, do you think that they will perish too? Your hope is set upon the world and your god is this life! You are corrupting your souls!
"Woe to you for the fire that burns in you, for it is insatiable!
"Woe to you because of the wheel that turns in your minds!"
(Thomas the Contender 143:11–17, NHL)

If we have ever experienced "the wheel that turns in our minds" and some of these other phrases, then maybe we, too, can relate to these sayings. Further along in the book it becomes clear where the struggle is taking place: "You are bound in caverns. . . . Your mind is deranged. . . .You darkened your hearts and surrendered your thoughts to folly . . . You walked by your own whims!" (Thomas the Contender 143:22, 29, 32, 144:2, NHL).

The continuities and extensions of the teachings of Jesus seem clear in *The Book of Thomas the Contender*. There are also some serious discontinuities. For example: "Woe to you who love intimacy with womankind and polluted intercourse with it!" (Thomas the Contender 144:9, NHL). Chalk this one up to the writer of Thomas the Contender's own inner battles.

Jesus includes women in his closest circle of friends and incorporates their experiences into his teachings. He ignores the barriers between men and women that were common in the culture of his time. There is nothing in his life or teachings similar to this line warning men about intimacy with women or calling intercourse polluted!

As we read this book, we might ask, "With whom is Thomas contending: his twin brother, other people, forces within himself, or all three?" Often our own inner conflicts, especially the unconscious ones, are the driving force for our outer conflicts with other people.

Now for a word of caution: in *The Book of Thomas the Contender*, as with all the documents containing accounts of experiences with the Resurrected Jesus, we may learn more about the people who wrote the documents than about what Jesus taught. Even so, I believe it is worth reading about their experiences for some of their struggles may illuminate some of our own.

Notes

2. Searching for the Parents of the Historic Jesus

1. See Appendix A for a discussion of the mythic meaning of the birth stories.

2. In attempting to identify the members of the historic family of Jesus, I want to acknowledge a debt of gratitude to the work of Robert Eisenman in his book *James the Brother of Jesus* (New York: Viking Press, 1997), in which he quite carefully uncovers the ways in which historic truth may have been obscured by mythic truth, especially by Jerome.

3. Eisenman, *James*, p. 840.

4. Origen's Commentaries in *The Ante Nicene Fathers* (Grand Rapids: Eerdmans,1980), vol. 10, p. 300.

3. James, Oldest Brother of Jesus

1. Josephus, *Antiquities of the Jews*, book XX, Chapter IX, 1, found in William Whiston, *Josephus, Complete Works* (Grand Rapids: Kregel Publications, 1960), p. 423.

2. Eusebius, *Ecclesiastical History,* XIX, trans. J. E. L. Oulton, Loeb Classical Library, vol. 2 (Cambridge: Harvard University Press, 1980), p. 177.

3. *Gospel of the Hebrews*, trans. Jerome, *De viris inlustris* 2, found in Ron Cameron, *The Other Gospels* (Philadelphia: Westminster Press, 1982), p. 177.

4. Thomas, Twin Brother of Jesus?

1. From the *Catecheses* by John Chrysostom, bishop, as reprinted in Howard Galley, *The Prayer Book Office* (New York: Harper & Row, Seabury Press, 1988), p. 733.

2. *Acts of Thomas*, 39, in *New Testament Apocrypha,* revised edition, vol. 2, Wilhelm Schneemelcher (Louisville: Westminister John Knox, 1992).

3. (From p. 37) I discuss *The Book of Thomas the Contender* in more detail in Appendix E.

5. Salome, Sister of Jesus

1. Mark 16:8. I want to thank Willis Barnstone for the opportunity to read a pre-publication copy of *Markos.*

6. Mourners Gathering in the Family Home

1. Pentecost was originally an agricultural feast celebrating the grain harvest seven weeks after Passsover. Just as Passover celebrated the freedom of the Israelites from bondage in Egypt, so Pentecost became a celebration of the giving of the Commandments to Moses on Mt. Sinai.

2. For a carefully reasoned discussion of how the election of Matthias is in the place where the selection of James belongs, consult Robert Eisenman, *James the Brother of Jesus* (New York: Viking Press, 1997), pp. 187, 265, 412–13.

9. Mary Magdalene and Teachings from the Resurrected Jesus

1. For a discussion of the dialogue between Mary Magdalene and her soul, see Appendix C.

10. Joanna's Peak Experience

1. Carla Ricci, *Mary Magdalene and Many Others* (Minneapolis, Fortress Press: 1994), pp. 159–60.

11. You Went Away and Left Us!

1. The numbering for *The Secret Book of James* will differ according to your translation. In the Nag Hammadi Library, bold-type numbers refer to pages in the documents, and numbers refer to lines on those pages. In the Scholars Version in the *Complete Gospels*, the Jesus Seminar scholars have provided us with convenient chapter and verse numbers.

14. Resurrected Jesus as Physician

1. *The Anchor Bible Dictionary* (New York: Doubleday, 1992), vol. 2, p. 806.

2. Burton, Thomas, *Serpent Handling Believers* (Nashville: University of Tennessee Press, 1993).

15. Resurrected Jesus as Child, Young Person, Servant, Old Man

1. At the time of Jesus and Paul, people often felt that there is a correlation between what is within a human being and what is beyond in the cosmos. This means that stories of moving through the several heavens can also mean moving through the energy centers of the body.

In the symbolic chakra system, each of us has seven energy centers within our bodies. The first chakra is located at the base of our spine, and the seventh is at the crown of the head, with the others located at specific locations in between. Just above the head is the eighth, farther out is the ninth, and way out in space is the ultimate tenth. In *The Discourse on the Eighth and Ninth* (NHL), a guide leads a seeker into these levels of spiritual ecstasy.

In Paul's own account, his energy is raised only to the third which is the chakra of Power. In reading his writings, sometimes it appears that his spiritual energy was arrested there as he became locked into power issues.

In this later story, Paul moves through the gates of the seven heavens (chakras) and then through the three beyond his body into the farthest reaches. Was Paul experiencing what is sometimes called an "out of the body experience"?

Those who believe in a soul separate from a body might interpret Paul's experience as a form of "astral traveling." Those of us who think of ourselves as more holistic would affirm the unity of body and soul; we are bodies, and when we are turned on we have soul. All experiences of "traveling" occur right here, right now, and within one's body, not outside of it. Even so, one can remain very much in the body and at the same time feel as though one is soaring into space. Some of us have such experiences as a result of intense prayer and meditation.

2. See chapter 8, "The Great Name of God," in Leo Schaya, *The Universal Meaning of the Kabbalah* (Baltimore: Penguin Books, 1974), pp. 151ff.

16. Ascending into the Heavens

1. T. W. Doane, *Bible Myths and Their Parallels in Other Religions* (New Hyde Park, N.Y.: University Books, 1971), pp. 215–32.

2. *Acts of Andrew*, found in Wilhelm Schneemelcher and R. McL. Wilson, trans., *New Testament Apocrypha* (Philadelphia: Westminster Press, 1964), vol. 2, pp. 418–19.

17. Sharing Resurrection Through Writing and Singing

1. For more information on the *The Q Gospel*, check the titles I have listed at the back of this book under the heading "For Further Reading and Study."

2. For dating and provenance of the *The Q Gospel and The Gospel of Thomas*,

see Robert Miller and the scholars of the Jesus Seminar, *The Complete Gospels* (Santa Rosa, Calif.: Polebridge Press, 1994), p. 6, and introductory notes to each Gospel.

3. Quotations are from *The Odes of Solomon* translated by Willis Barnstone.

Some are published in *The Other Bible,* Willis Barnstone (San Francisco, Calif.: Harper and Row, 1984). Others are not yet published but used with permission.

18. Bread Rising in Eucharistic Communities

1. *The Didache,* Cyril C. Richardson, trans. In *Early Christian Fathers*, vol. 1 (Philadelphia: Westminster Press, 1953).

2. The laver refers to the water and the washing of the person in baptism.

3. *The Apostolic Tradition of Hippolytus*, Burton Scott Easton, trans. (Ann Arbor: Archon Books, 1962).

4. *The Acts of John* is a third-century document probably written in Syria or Asia Minor. An English translation is included in Wilhelm Schneemelcher and R. McL. Wilson, trans., *New Testament Apocrypha*, 2 vols. (Louisville: Westminster/John Knox Press, 1990).

19. Experiencing Resurrection Through Baptism

1. I grew up with the idea that Jesus didn't really need to be baptized because he was already perfect. The purpose of his baptism was an example to us, that we should be baptized. But shortly after I turned thirty-three, I began going to Four Springs for seminars of the Guild for Psychological Studies led by Dr. Elizabeth Howes; she raised many startling and creative questions for me. Among the most powerful were those she raised in connection with the baptism of Jesus when she asked, "What might have been happening inside Jesus?"

If Jesus doesn't need to be baptized, then is he just going through the motions? Following that line of thought, his baptism begins to ring rather hollow. I assume the honesty of Jesus, and I cannot stand the idea that he would do anything just for outer appearances. The result is that I am forced to ask, very deeply in my soul, what might have been going on within Jesus during his baptism?

2. For a discussion on the virgin birth stories, see Appendix A.

3. *The Acts of Thomas*, Harold Attridge, trans., pending publication by Polebridge Press, Santa Rosa, California.

20. Time Out in the Wilderness

1. *The Sibylline Oracles* is a collection of spiritual songs by anonymous authors living and singing in Syria, Egypt, and Asia Minor during the first three centuries of the Common Era. This particular song, a hymn to Christ, may have originated in the Jordan Valley.

2. *"The two begotten from each other's sides"* is a reference to Adam and Eve. Sybil asserts that Adam and Eve see the coming of Christ and rejoice.

Appendix A. Virgin Birth Stories as Mythic Truth

1. Joseph Campbell defined myth in a lecture given at First Unitarian-Universalist Church, San Francisco, California, April 28, 1978.

Appendix B. Son of Man: Seed of True Humanity

1. If you choose to look up *Ezekiel* and read it yourself, please be careful in the translation you select. The best translations of *Ezekiel* are The Jerusalem Bible, The New Jerusalem Bible, and the first and second editions of the Revised Standard Version. These capture the richness and depth of the phrase "Son of Man." The New Revise Standard Version is overall a good translation, but it misses the point of the *Ezekiel* passage by rendering "Son of Man" as "Mortal."

Appendix C. Mary Magdelene's Dialogue with Her Soul

1. Neil Douglas-Klotz, *Prayers of the Cosmos* (San Francisco: Harper & Row, 1990), p. 23.

Thank You

Thank you for reading my book and considering some of the ideas and questions I may have raised for you. I take full responsibility for the eclectic arrangement of thoughts and feelings that appear on these pages. At the same time, I am eternally grateful to an enormous host of people who live deep within my soul. I want to express my heartfelt thanks to them.

Thank you Jesus, Mary Magdalene, and the Resurrected Jesus in all your wondrous manifestations. My primary thanks go to you and to that unfathomable mystery who is within, around, and beyond us. From you, the miracle of life and all blessings flow, including the following people who continue to make enormous impact on me in gently powerful ways:

All the writers of the Gospels and other Holy Scriptures, together with the translators, historians, and scholars who convey to us vital information on the experience of the Resurrected Jesus in the first three centuries.

Lao Tsu, the Old Wise One, who provides me with the Taoist Way and keeps teaching me over and over to hold the opposites in balance.

Socrates and his student Plato, who reveal that only in dialogue is Wisdom found.

George Berkeley, philosopher bishop, who provides the motto for Berkeley Divinity School, my seminary, "*In illa quae ultra sunt,*" "Into that which is beyond."

Carl Gustav Jung, whose psychology embraces all the archetypes who live in the depths of the unconscious, including death, entombment, resurrection, and ascension.

Joseph Campbell, who stimulates some of my persistent questions, including: What are the myths that people will live by in the twenty-first century? Which myths of the past have died, and which ones are still vital for us when we are in touch with them?

Frederick C. Wood Jr., who first opened my mind to the possibilities of a nonliteral understanding of resurrection by asking, "Which body rose?" Fred died not long after his book, *Living in the Now*, was published, but the insights of his book continue to enlighten my understanding.

Char Matejovski and her husband, Robert Funk, plus all the scholars of the Jesus Seminar and Westar Institute, whose research and publishing provide me with essential tools for my own study. I start with Char because she is the one who, once the scholars have made their decisions, does the painstaking work of entering the data and putting it into publishable format.

Karen L. King, Harvard scholar, whose writings, seminars, translations, and work on *The Gospel of Mary* take me further into this exciting text and the seed of the true humanity.

Robert Eisenman, whose careful and painstaking research in *James the Brother of Jesus* has enabled me to rediscover the family of Jesus.

John Painter, working simultaneously and independently of Eisenman, produced *Just James: The Brother of Jesus in History and Tradition*.

Elizabeth Boyden Howes, whose passion for Jesus helps keep my own passion burning and focused on the person of Jesus and the mythic dimension in the Gospel records and other Holy Scriptures. Her seminars on *The Records of Jesus*, which she led at Four Springs, have made profound changes in my life and have provided me with the tools I need for my own inner work.

Robert Lentz, whose soul creates icons of Spirit-filled people, including Mary Magdalene, Christ of the Desert, John Donne, Aelred, Gandhi, Thomas Merton, Francis and Clare, Teresa of Avila, John of the Cross, and Martin Luther King Jr. Robert's icons surround me as I work and give me windows into the soul of the Mystery of life.

William Edwin Swing, my bishop, who consistently encourages my explorations in accordance with the Anglican motto taken from the Gospel of John that "The truth shall set you free."

The people of St. Peter's Episcopal Church, San Francisco, who were with me during intense times of research. The year after *The Nag Hammadi Library* was published in English in 1977, I became their priest and pastor. As I made new discoveries in this rich material, I told them what I was finding. Many were keenly interested. Even when they were baffled about what I was really trying to say, their love for me and mine for them kept us on a steady course together for over eighteen years. My time with St. Peter's laid the groundwork for this book.

Antonnette Vaglia Graham, whose intense reactions and constructive criticism of an earlier draft resulted in a significantly reshaped manuscript.

Patrick Andersen, whose careful reading and attention to detail caught many typos and glitches and raised substantive questions for change.

Henry Carrigan, Editorial Director of Trinity Press International, who accepted my manuscript for publication, gave it an appropriate title, and provided me with the editorial guidance I needed for completing the book.

Grace Vilez, my greatest critic and my most loving wife, who follows the thought processes and complex labyrinths of my mind. She is the one who gave me the phrase "within, around, and beyond." She chooses to share daily life with me, travels with me on many of my searching ventures, and keeps introducing me to Mysteries right in plain view. Grace reminds me to "Be here now" and savor what I already have. When I am totally absorbed in work at the computer, Grace will come into my study and ask, "Would you like a cup of tea or coffee?" I often reply, "Yes!" which prompts her to clarify by asking, "Which?"

All my opponents and adversaries who, in countless ways, help shape my life and thinking expressed in this book.

All those scholars and writers whose books surround me in my study and whose work I consult regularly. In preparing this book, I especially appreciate those writers whose books I list for you in my next section. If what I have written sparks or rekindles your own interest, you may want to consider some of these reading suggestions.

For Further Reading
and Study

Resurrection Stories

Miller, Robert J.. ed. *The Complete Gospels*. Santa Rosa: Polebridge Press, 1992.
    See especially: Gospel of Mark16; Gospel of Matthew 28; Gospel of Luke
    24; Gospel of John 20–21; Gospel of Mary; Secret Book of James.
Robinson, James M., gen. ed. *The Nag Hammadi Library in English*. San Francisco:
    Harper & Row, first edition 1977; third edition 1988. See especially:
    Apocryphon of James; Apocryphon of John; Book of Thomas the Contender;
    Sophia of Jesus Christ; Apocalypse of Paul; First Apocalypse of James; Second
    Apocalypse of James; Acts of Peter and the Twelve Apostles; Second Treatise of
    the Great Seth;Apocalypse of Peter; Letter of Peter to Philip; Gospel of Mary.
Schneemelcher, Wilhelm, and R. McL. Wilson. trans. *New Testament Apocrypha*.
    2 vols. Louisville: Westminster/John Knox Press, 1990. A rich compendium
    and most valuable resource. For serious students this is a gold mine.

The Lost Gospel of Q

Borg, Marcus, Mark Powelson, and Ray Riegert, eds. *The Lost Gospel Q: The
    Original Sayings of Jesus*. Berkeley: Ulysses Press, 1996.
Kloppenborg, John S. *Q Parallels*. Santa Rosa: Polebridge Press, 1988.
Kloppenborg, John S., Marvin W. Meyer, Stephen J. Patterson, and Michael
    G. Steinhauser. *Q Thomas Reader*. Santa Rosa: Polebridge Press, 1990.
Mack, Burton L. *The Lost Gospel: The Book of Q and Christian Origins*. San
    Francisco: HarperSanFrancisco, 1993.

Jesus

Sanford, John A. *The Kingdom Within*. Philadelphia: Lippincott, 1970.
——. Mystical Christianity. New York: Crossroad, 1995.

The following books on Jesus are available from the Guild for Psychological Studies Publishing House, P.O. Box 29385, San Francisco, CA 94129–0385.

Guild for Psychological Studies. *Questions for a Seventeen-Day Seminar Based on the Synoptic Gospels*. San Francisco: Guild Publishing, 1998.

Howes, Elizabeth Boyden, and Sheila Moon. *Intersection and Beyond*. 2 vols. San Francisco: Guild Publishing, 1971, 1986.

——. *Jesus' Answer to God*. San Francisco: Guild Publishing, 1984.

——. *The Choicemaker*. Wheaton, Il.: Quest Books, 1973.

Sharman, Henry Burton. *Records of the Life of Jesus*. San Francisco: Guild Publishing, 1991.

Wink, Walter. *Transforming Bible Study*. Nashville: Abingdon Press, 1992.

The Resurrected Jesus

Dalai Lama. *The Good Heart*. Boston: Wisdom Publications, 1996.

Dart, John. *The Laughing Savior*. San Francisco: Harper & Row, 1976.

Fox, Matthew. *The Coming of the Cosmic Christ*. San Francisco: Harper & Row, 1980.

Hanh, Thich Nhat. *Going Home: Jesus and Buddha as Brothers*. New York: Riverhead Books, 1999.

——. *Living Buddha, Living Christ*. New York: Riverhead Books, 1995.

Spong, John Shelby. *Resurrection: Myth or Reality?* San Francisco: HarperSan Francisco, 1994.

Mary Magdalene and the Other Women

de Boer, Esther. *Mary Magdalene, Beyond the Myth*. Harrisburg, Pa.: Trinity Press International, 1997.

Haskins, Susan. *Mary Magdalen: Myth and Metaphor*. New York: Harcourt Brace, 1993.

Moltmann-Wendel, Elizabeth. *The Women Around Jesus*. New York: Crossroad, 1990.

Ricci, Carla. *Mary Magdalene and Many Others*. Minneapolis: Fortress Press, 1994.

Schüssler Fiorenza, Elisabeth. *In Memory of Her*. New York: Crossroad, 1985.

Starbird, Margaret. *The Woman with the Alabaster Jar*. Santa Fe: Bear & Co., 1993.

James the Brother of Jesus

Eisenman, Robert. *James the Brother of Jesus*. New York: Viking Press, 1997.
Painter, John. *Just James: The Brother of Jesus in History and Tradition.* Columbia, S.C.: University of South Carolina Press, 1997.

Son of Man (Seed of the True Humanity)

Borsch, Frederick Houk. *The Son of Man in Myth and History*. Philadelphia: Westminster Press, 1967.
Harvey, Andrew. *Son of Man*. New York: Tarcher Putnam, 1998.
Howes, Elizabeth Boyden. "Son of Man—Expression of Self." In *Intersection and Beyond*. San Francisco: Guild for Psychological Studies, 1971.
Wink, Walter. "Son of Man." In *The Once and Future Jesus*. Santa Rosa: The Jesus Seminar, Westar Institute, 2000.

Praying, Baptizing, Anointing with the Spirit, and Eucharistic Celebrations

Dix, Gregory, and Henry Chadwick. *The Treatise on the Apostolic Tradition of St. Hippolytus of Rome*. London: Alban Press, 1992.
Easton, Burton Scott. *The Apostolic Tradition of Hippolytus*. Ann Arbor, Mich.: Archon Books, 1962.
Robinson, James M.. *The Nag Hammadi Library in English*. San Francisco: Harper & Row, first edition 1977, third edition 1988. See especially: Prayer of the Apostle Paul; Gospel of Philip; Thunder, Perfect Mind; Discourse on the Eighth and Ninth; Prayer of Thanksgiving.

Jesus and Jung
Seminar Centers

When you are ready to take some time out for personal growth and inner work, you might consider contacting Four Springs Seminars and the Guild for Psychological Studies. Both seminar centers seek to integrate the life and teachings of Jesus as found in the Gospels with insights from the depth psychology of Carl Gustav Jung.

In addition, arrangements can be made with the author, John Beverley Butcher, for seminars to be given in your area.

Four Springs Seminars

Four Springs has been a home to spiritual and psychological exploration for more than forty years. The genesis of the work at Four Springs has been in mining texts related to the life of Jesus with the tools of analytical psychology, and many seminars retain a focus on what each participant may discover at the intersection of depth psychology and a fresh encounter with these texts. Seminars at Four Springs also draw regularly upon the rich resources of wisdom and myth from other traditions, and the nonverbal learning that takes place through expression in art and drama, music and silence.

This approach has roots in the work of Henry Burton Sharman, who developed questions for groups to explore the Gospel accounts for clues to Jesus' own religious experience. Sharman's questions were designed to help people discern Jesus' self-estimate from the beliefs of those who recorded his life and teachings. Sharman's unique arrangement of the Gospels for comparative study was published as *Records of the Life of Jesus*. In the 1930s, one of Sharman's students, Elizabeth Boyden Howes, began to lead Records studies in California, later finding colleagues in Sheila Moon and Luella Sibbald. Together they expanded upon Sharman's approach through their relationship with C. G. Jung, the study of myth, and the integration of experiential techniques.

Howes, Moon, and Sibbald founded the Guild for Psychological Studies and established their work at Four Springs—in 1955. From these origins and with the creative effort of Guild leaders and seminar participants, a unique seminar method has evolved at Four Springs: a method centered on questions designed to allow participants a living encounter between themselves and a text, and making use of movement, music, drama, and individual expression in art. Four Springs itself has evolved as a seminar site, its natural beauty enhanced by this work and the soulful labor of many people over the years.

Four Springs Seminars was created in 1996 to serve the distinctive form of educational experience that takes place at Four Springs. In addition to offering seminars that build upon the traditions established here, Four Springs Seminars works with the Guild for Psychological Studies and hosts other events that touch upon the integration of psychological perspectives and the religious dimension of human experience.

Two hours north of San Francisco by automobile, Four Springs is secluded on nearly three hundred acres of oak, madrone, and mixed conifer forest in the foothills of the Mayacamas Mountains in southern Lake County. Natural springs on the property provide clear, refreshing water.

Seminars are small in size, leaving room for participants to encounter a topic and to explore life, both as it is expressed in nature and as it lives within. The lodge, cabins, art, and meditation buildings, the library and the seminar room, together with the pool, grape arbor, meadows, and trails combine to create an opening in the midst of daily concerns. Here we may take nourishment for inner possibilities that otherwise might go unnoticed.

Away from daily routines and close to nature, we can more easily observe how the earth provides a home for us, offers beauty at every step, and is filled with mystery beyond our understanding.

In addition to the seminars that are offered, a small number of cabins are available on occasion for individual retreat or study leave. To receive information and current brochure, contact Four Springs Seminars, 14598 Sheveland Road, Middletown, CA 95461: 707–987-4510; info@foursprings.org.

The Guild for Psychological Studies

The Guild for Psychological Studies has for over fifty years grappled with the problems of each decade. Such goals seem more urgent than ever before as we begin a new century. Using material from psychology, mythology, religion, and the arts, a framework is provided within which individuals may be aided in their search for their own highest values and deepest awareness through a better understanding of their unconscious and conscious processes. A principal course of study has been a fresh approach to the teachings of the man Jesus, using principles of the analytical psychology of Carl Gustav Jung. A method of group discussion, with evocative questions and individual responses, is used for a more personal approach to the values found in the various texts studied.

The work of the Guild is founded on two basic convictions: that there is an increasing need for the practical and historical applications of inner experience and psychological insights; and that there is also need for redefinitions of the words *psychological* and *religious spirit* in people as major and interdependent personality factors.

The term *guild* is used in the wide sense of a group of persons working together at generally shared purposes. Based on these purposes and convictions, the Guild program includes winter seminars at Four Springs and at sites in the San Francisco Bay Area and other cities.

Academic knowledge of psychology and religion is not a prerequisite for the seminars, and mere intellectual understanding of texts and concepts is not the goal. Rather, the assumption is that concepts are and should be workable, and the approach is designed to assist individuals in their own unique search, relevant to each day's experience.

This search includes the discovery of new meaning in ourselves and others, and implies that there are practical means available—instruments with which to overcome that which distorts our perspective, deadens relationships, and cuts us off from the sources of new life. With these tools we can approach, begin to understand, accept, and come to terms with those parts and processes in ourselves that lie beyond the boundaries of consciousness, but nonetheless have enormously dynamic potential and significance.

The outcome of this search by individuals for their own total value has been variously expressed by people of all ages, all cultures: by religious leaders, poets, philosophers, and in our time by scientists. They have used such expressions as the *inner light, the divine spark, the Kingdom of God within, the Self,* or such terms as *self-actualization, wholeness, individuation,* and the *integration of the personality.*

Seminar method: In discussion sessions, the seminar leader asks questions intended to evoke responses on the part of all questions designed to illumine the meaning the text offers to us. Because there is no single "right" answer to such questions, individuals are encouraged to think for themselves, to consult their own resources, and to contribute their own unique response to the material, as free of preconceptions as possible. They are also encouraged to listen with genuine openness to other contributions. There is no need and no attempt to reach any group agreement. During other periods of the day, seminar work is augmented by art, movement, and ritual.

For information and current brochure, contact The Guild for Psychological Studies, P.O. Box 29385, San Francisco, CA 94129-0385: voice 415-561-2385; fax 415-931-1273; email guildsf@aol.com; web site www.guildsf.org.

About the Author

John Beverley Butcher is a priest of the Episcopal Diocese of California who has served Arizona and California churches. His primary commitment is in seeking ways of becoming more authentically human by focusing on the experience of Jesus. His writing and seminars seek to integrate Holy Scripture, archetypal psychology, Taoist philosophy, and personal experience. He has been leading seminars in the San Francisco Bay area and throughout the country since 1976.

He is the son of Harold Butcher, an English freelance journalist and lecturer, and Elizabeth Ford, an American musician and teacher. He was raised in Prescott, Arizona, earned his Bachelor of Arts in Philosophy and Psychology from Harvard and his Master of Divinity from Berkeley Divinity School at Yale. His continuing education includes work at the Graduate Theological Union, Berkeley, California, and seminars with the Guild for Psychological Studies in San Francisco and Four Springs, a retreat center in Lake County just outside Middletown, California. He is a Fellow of the Canadian College for Chinese Studies.

His first book, *The Tao of Jesus*, a Book of Days for the Natural Year, was published by HarperSan Francisco in 1994.

Seminars in Your Area

The author is available for seminars and lectures expanding the material in this book and on other topics. For information and current brochure, contact: The Rev. John Beverley Butcher, 228 Hedge Road, Menlo Park, CA 94025: Phone 650-321-0887; email JBBNOW@aol.com.